You Deserve To Be a Millionaire

By Fabian Avila

All Rights Reserved
Copyright 2019

Prologue:

Most of the people in this world today, dream big with becoming a Millionaire one day. They all want to join the Millionaire or the Billionaire clubs, somehow. Of course, they all want those achievements to be made, in "Dollars" or "Euros" bills, or higher denominations. And most of the people around the world would also like to achieve this goal, in the least amount of time as possible.

A lot of people in this world have also been able to make those millions, or billions, for themselves. They are a selected group of the "Self Made" millionaires, or billionaires, who have somehow, by the use of their knowledge, talents, skills, hard work, discipline, charisma and virtue, achieved and fulfilled all their financial dreams. They are rich, filthy rich, and a lot of them have achieved that status by themselves, all within their lifetimes. Becoming a great example of perseverance, hard work, intelligence, admiration, sometimes luck and a lot of success.

Of course, there are a lot of successful people in this world, also, who have obtained their wealth by the beautiful luck of having being born into a wealthy family. In fact, most of the rich people in this world, have obtained their wealth, via this fashion. Because of their beautiful luck, of being born into a wealthy family, they have had the privilege to receive a significant amount of access to a large amount of family fortune and wealth. And by all means, they all deserve to be rich and wealthy as well. Especially if they are able to, or they have been able to, grow and multiply their fortune and make it bigger for themselves and their generations to come.   That seems to be their inherited responsibility, to become wealthier if they can.

Niccolo Machiavelli, a prolific and influential roman writer and diplomat from the 16th century, author of the book "The Prince," had a fascinating argument in which he contrasted the notions of "Virtue vs. Fortune" in one of his books. Two very unique nouns that could be useful to describe the difference between the self-made millionaire, and those millionaires who have inherited all their money. By Virtue, Machiavelli refereed "to the skill and temperament of the prince"[1], in this case, the self-made millionaire, used to achieve its self-fulfilling role. The self-made millionaire required a lot of virtues to achieve that status, which includes among many others, the virtues of discipline, commitment, resilience, intelligence, sacrifice, and guts. And by fortune, on the other hand, Machiavelli meant; "essentially what we would think of as the role of luck"[2] in today's day and age. Meaning, those who inherited the money, were mostly lucky, or fortunate. But they also needed to develop and possess the virtues of the self-made millionaire, in order to maintain or increase their wealth.

In that sense, there are those self-made millionaires who have achieved their wealth by means of their own virtue. And there are those who have inherited their money by means of luck or fortune. Of course, under all circumstances, they are all wealthy, and they all deserve to be wealthy and filthy rich. Furthermore, they all have the capacity and responsibility to grow or increase their wealth. Therefore, this book focuses on that end. To offer its readers the principles, tactics, and strategies to build, maintain and grow their wealth and capital to a larger scale.

Therefore, this book was written for everyone, people from all shapes, forms, and ages. But with particular attention to all of those individuals who think or believe that they deserve to be millionaires. This includes the virtuous self-made millionaire, the fortunate wealthy people who inherited millions by means of love and luck and those who want to become millionaires by the process of discovering a few secrets about how rich people obtained their millions in the first place.

Because in the end, wealth management and capital creation is all about maintaining your economic resources, but also about multiplying them and transforming them into more wealth. Whether if you were given a head start by the fortunes of life or if you want to become a self-made millionaire, we all have, if healthy, all the abilities, opportunities and capacities to multiply our economic resources and turn them into millions or billions of dollars. That is if we apply the right principles, tactics, and strategies at the right point of time. Yes, you can also become millionaires or billionaires, but only, if we are passionate and intelligent about that end.

Time is money, so in an effort to value your time and attention when you read this book, I will go straight to the point, about what kind of information and other resources you will find in this book. Whether if you were lucky enough to be born in a wealthy, or filthy rich family, or whether if you are a self-made millionaire. Even if you are not a millionaire yet, but believe that you deserve to be a Millionaire. You will find some of the strategies, tactics, and principles that will allow you to create and multiply your wealth in this book but also to maintain it.

There are eleven principles in this book that you will have to understand, in order for you to build, sustain and scale your wealth. Whether if you are already filthy rich right now, or whether if you are just starting; the first step is to think and act like a millionaire is to master the process of wealth accumulation.

BOOK CHAPTERS

Chapter 1

Master the Art of Real Estate Investment

The main reason why I begin this book, with a Real Estate Chapter, is because Real Estate has always been one of the most effective and secure ways to begin the process of wealth accumulation. After all, just the process of buying your first home and starting to build equity on your mortgage is a good step towards saving money over the long term. So the process of starting to build your own real estate portfolio, whether if it is residential or commercial, it's crucial to begin your process of wealth creation and to begin to think and act like a millionaire. Of course, in order for you to become a millionaire, one, two, three or even four houses are not going to get you there. The reality is that for you to really become a millionaire, in whatever type of business you are or operate, you need to scale it up to the masses, but this is something we'll talk about to a greater extent in a few paragraphs ahead.

However, if you are just beginning the process of wealth accumulation, real estate is the safest, most secure, proven and reliable method to build and sustain wealth. If not, think about all the Kings and Queens from around the world, or even the same Donald Trump, who is a Real Estate Magnate. The one thing they all have in common is that they all have, possess or manage a lot of lands. And let me remind you, a good piece of land, will always give you a good return of investment. They say that money does not grow in trees. Well, you'll think differently if the trees that grow on your farm give you avocados, and you sell them for a profit in the market place.

So, therefore, it is safe to say that Real Estate is always an excellent place to begin your wealth creation journey. Of course, there are a lot of other principles of the wealth creation process, that need to be added into this formula in order for you to be successful in the Real Estate business, but overall, Real Estate is a good place for you to start. The principle of arbitrage, for instance, can also be applied into the Real Estate business, or every business you may encounter as a matter of fact, because the principle of arbitrage, will always give you profit if you apply it correctly in most business settings.

According to Drew Levin and Kevin O Leary, from Shark Tank, "In real estate; your money will always be made in the buy of the property." And that it's always nearly true for every business. You will always make the money for any product, or service when you buy it at a low price, and then sell it at a much higher price.

To explain the process of arbitrage in greater detail, the principle of "Arbitrage" is basically the process of buying a product or service for a low price, and then selling it for a higher price to someone else, hopefully at the same time. This principle is applied in the stock and the foreign exchange markets, but also on the e-commerce market, via the use of a "drop shipping" strategy, where you sell something for a higher price in your amazon.com store, or your own personal e-commerce store and buy it at a lower price from Alibaba.com in China, almost immediately, using the inventory of the alibaba.com e-commerce store to fulfill that order. You can make this profitable business transaction, without even having to keep any inventories at hand, or in your physical store, but simply, by using the inventory of the alibaba.com e-commerce store. In a way, you serve just as the middleman taking advantage of the price difference between two products in two different market places. That is how you make your profit. We'll explain later on, the full concept of drop shipping, but for now let's just stick to arbitrage and real estate, so that we don't get out of track in this money making endeavor.

Arbitrage is defined as "the practice of taking advantage of a price difference between two or more markets [or products]: striking a combination of matching deals that capitalize upon the imbalance [of price], the profit made is the difference between the market prices." Like we said before, in more simple terms, arbitrage simply means to buy low and sell high.

Principle #1

Arbitrage = BUY LOW > SELL HIGH

In the real estate market, for instance, you can apply this principle of buying low and selling high, by purchasing a house in the foreclosure market, or by purchasing a home in a bad condition and then flip in it, (meaning, fixing the house and selling it for a higher price for a profit at a later date, once the house has been fixed). Or you can use this **arbitrage tactic** by simply buying a property from a seriously distressed seller, and selling it on a later date at market value for a higher price.

A **distressed seller** is someone who is desperate to sell their house, for any given reason, even if they lose some money in the process. Whether if the homeowners are moving to a different state, or they just got, or they can't simply make the mortgage payments, or the political conditions of the locality where they live are not favorable to them, and they just want to move out their neighborhood. Those are all distressed sellers, and trust me there are a lot of those individuals, or deals in the market place. People who just want to get rid of their houses and sell them.

An example of how to buy from a distressed seller:

House "A" is valued at USD 500,000.00 in the market place. Because the husband passed away a few months ago, the house is placed on sale. The widow does not want to live in that house anymore. The house had not been sold for a few months, and the seller is tired of the property. She is willing to sell the house for USD 450,000.00. You are the potential buyer, and you offer them USD 420,000.00 for the property. The seller accepts. By knowing how to negotiate correctly, you have made your self a profit of $80,000.00 in one simple transaction.

Trust me; in this one and all distress buying scenarios, you are not taking advantage of the seller, you are just offering a solution to their problems. They need the money right now, for whatever reason. Maybe the widow in this case just wants to travel the world. Or move in with her daughters and sons as soon as possible. You are giving them the solution, which is cash, for an actual problem the seller had. In this case, it is an unwanted property. You take their property and make a profit, in exchange. The truth is that there are a lot of real estate experts out there who only specialize in this process of buying properties from distressed owners. The key here is to try to buy the property, at the lowest possible price, so that you can make a profit in the purchase of the house.

You can also buy foreclosure properties from the banks. A foreclosure in real estate happens when "a lender, either private or traditional, take back the real estate they financed from the borrower due to non-payment." But in order for them to sell those properties, they need to put them in an auction. Therefore, it is better to negotiate with cash this auction property transactions, because there will always be a lot of competitors bidding for those properties, but also, because these transactions need to be made fast. A loan processing takes time, and it usually requires a few weeks or more in order to get completed, and these type auction transactions, all happen in less than a five days window. So you must act fast if you want to cash into this fabulous opportunity.

The key here, as we have continuously repeat it in this chapter, is to put in practice the principle number one of this book, of commerce negotiation, business transactions and the wealth creation process and that is, to buy low, and sell high whatever type of product or service, you are negotiating with.

First Home or Deal Scenario:

If you are in the beginning stages of your wealth accumulation process and you want to invest in the real estate market, always remember principle number one of the wealth creation process, which is to buy low and sell high. Of course, if you have a limited budget, and are considering to buying a house for the first time, for equity building and as a first investment solution, think about buying first a multifamily unit. The main reason, why I suggest multifamily units, is because, with the rent of one of your units, you can possibly pay the entire mortgage of your entire property. Making the property pay for itself. In that sense, you'll begin to understand the process of real estate investment, not only from the buyer's perspective but also from the landlord perspective.

One of the most important channels for cash flow and revenue that most of the advanced Real Estate Investors use in this industry is the business model of renting their units, mostly at a large scale.

Most multimillionaire real estate investors buy and sell, apartment complexes with a very minimum of 16 units per complex so that they can make a profit out of renting those units. If they rent all the 16 units, they will be making a profit and net income over their investments. If they rent only eight or nine of those sixteen units, they'll be making a break even on their investment, meaning; their investment will pay for itself. Any additional rental revenue after the eight or nine-unit will be considered as profit and hopefully, it will become net income for the investor.

Therefore, when you buy your first home, it is essential, if you want later on to scale up your investments in the first place, to begin with, the process of buying multifamily properties. Whether if you buy a two, three or four units, multifamily property, this property will give you the foundation to start building wealth and positive cash flow, while the property pays for itself.

For example, let's pretend that you just bought a four units multifamily property for USD 600,000.00. Let's say that your mortgage payment for the loan is 1670.00 USD per month. If you rent three of the four units, at 750.00 dollars a month, you will be making $2250.00 a month. With that money, you will pay for the full monthly mortgage itself, some of the utilities and operation cost of your building maintenance per month, and hopefully, you will get a profit. Furthermore, you'll be able to live for free in your fourth unit, because the other three unit rental payments will cover the fourth unit where you live. You will also be making cash flow revenue from this property, maybe in the two to three hundred dollars value per month.

Furthermore, let us remember that under favorable conditions, all houses increase their value over time. So, if in three years, your multifamily property, is valued at $900,000.00. You would have made a profit, or wealth gain of an additional USD 300,000.00 in your wealth portfolio value.

On the contrary, if you decide to buy only one residential house, without units for rental available at a USD 600000.00 price, you will have to cover the entire mortgage payment for your self, without gaining any profit, or cash flow from the unit. Besides, the equity and value gained of the property over the years will be slow. Furthermore, the process of wealth creation via this method cannot be scalable. Therefore, you will not become rich via this method, and your mortgage interest will take a lot of your valued money from you. Consequently, we do not recommend this method, if you want to become a millionaire.

The truth is that some of the wealthiest Real Estate Moguls inside the United States such as Grant Cardone, and even Donald Trump as mentioned before, have more than a hundred apartment complexes, under their portfolios, managing at the very minimum, at least 1000 units of rental unit properties, and most of them, already rented at full capacity. Yes, renting your real estate units is the way to go, so that when and if the numbers are right, you can make millions, if not, billions of dollars out of those investments.

Millionaire Portfolio Scenario:

Of course, one of the major principles for a safe, secure and balanced millionaire investment strategy, overall, includes the principle of portfolio diversification. In fact, according to Kevin O Leary, a well-known investor Millionaire from Shark Tank, "Portfolio Diversification" is a priority for him. In fact, he keeps 50% of his portfolio in Real Estate, for wealth maintenance and accumulation purposes, but also for safety. As we mentioned before, the Real Estate economic sector is one of the most secure sectors of all. The rest of his investment portfolio, he has diversified, even by economic sectors, so that if one sector of the economy falls short, his other investments will be secured.

His investment portfolio approach simply ratifies what we have been saying in this chapter. If you want peace of mind, it is better to invest in real estate. Let us considered Grant Cardone, for example. A self-made Real Estate Millionaire Mogul who lives in the city of Sunni Isles, Miami, Florida. He built his real estate empire from scratch at a mature age, but he did it through a multifamily property tactic, or approach. Of course, he became a multimillionaire by first *finding a system, or a formula, and then scaling it up and replicating it as much as possible*. By scaling it up, I mean, by investing in larger, more profitable margin making properties that required and were quantified by the millions of dollars. In other words, the same principle of a multifamily property approach mentioned in the first home buying scenario, but this time on a larger scale. Instead of a thousand of dollars transaction as many people who are making their first initial real estate investment do, Grand Cardone performs million dollar transactions. That is scaling it up.

Of course, for you to reach the millionaire level, not only do you need to have the knowledge and skills to perform this kind of transactions successfully, but you also need to have the investment capacity to make these kinds of deals. Of course, there is also a methodology and processes to the madness. And you need to have money to make money. A lot of these millionaire investors, however, have also another set of valuable attributes and skills that help them achieve these goals. For instance, they are all great communicators and negotiators. They also possess a great deal of persuasion and selling skills. Each one of them, for example, has their own TV Shows. And what does a TV show does, we'll it takes the information to the masses. In other words, they escalate the reach of these mogul's messages to a broader audience. Sometimes even to a global audience. Take Kevin O' Leary and his successful TV Show "Shark Tank," or take the example of Donald Trump and his successful TV Show "The Apprentice." Why do you think Donald Trump is the 45th president of the United States of America? Simple; because everyone in the world knows him. Or even take Grand Cardone and his Youtube.com channel. Did you know that Youtube.com users have reached the 1,300,000,000 marks worldwide and that nearly 5 billion videos were watched in the Youtube.com platform in the year 2018?

Therefore, whether if these magnates are showcased in the mainstream media or via their own youtube.com channels and other social media platforms, these millionaire leaders are expert communicators, marketers, and persuasive sellers who understand the impact of digital marketing, mass communications, publicity, and advertisement. That is why they have a large number of products and services available for sale at any given point in time via all of these channels. Yes, they are full throttle capitalist, and they love it, but most of it;

they all deserve to be millionaires and billionaires because they know how to make money.

Let us not forget; however, that Real Estate is the backbone of their wealth. That is their money making machine. In that sense, if you have learned to play the game of monopoly in real life, the chances are that you own a few houses, hotels, apartment complexes and another real estate commercial property that has made you, or is making you a millionaire. But for you to really become a Billionaire, you need to learn how to scale up your business. And that takes us to principle number two of the wealth creation process, and that is the principle of scalability.

Principle # 2

SCALE-UP YOUR BUSINESS

If you nickel and dime your business, you are not going to become a millionaire. Not even in the real estate business. The reality is that you are going to have to deal with millions or even billion-dollar deals if you want to reach the millionaire or billionaire status. It is only from those types of large-scale investments, deals, and business transaction, where your apartment buildings, hotels, and real estate complexes will offer you the cash flow and revenue necessary so that you can begin to talk about being a millionaire, or billionaire.

If these deals are done correctly, with the right set of numbers, planning, and future projections analysis; the investor will win from the purchase. They will also obtain the cash flow and the profit gained from the time value of the property. By all means, however, if you really want to scale up your real estate business, you will have to begin to deal with million dollar transactions. But you are going to have to invest in real estate knowledge and do what the experts do, and you are going to have to do it well.

In fact, one of the biggest challenges you will find at this point of your business will be the issue of finding or raising the money or economic resources to complete these types of transactions. You will have to find a lot of different mechanisms and methods to reach these goals. Such as finding additional investors and sharing the revenue and the cost of the project with them, or you will have to seek private loans, and other types of funding opportunities to obtain the money. You may even have to put some of your own other properties as collateral, or you may have to undertake an IPO or initial public offering in one of your companies, if you have any, in order to raise funds. You can also find a strategic funding partner, as multiple real estate training company's offers out there.

Just as important in this process, will be to offer a very complete and detailed business plan about the project to those who may want to invest with you. This business plan will have to be very rigorous and will need to account for all the future money projections, break-even analysis, the history and conditions of the building and the market place where you are investing. The political conditions as well, of the locality where the investment will be made, will need to be revised, and all other detailed information that needs to be accounted for before making the deal will have to be placed in the table.

There are multiple tactics and techniques to build and accumulate wealth through real estate. After all, if you really think about it, the real estate market covers one of the most essential pillars of consumption in the market place, and that is shelter. People need to eat first, and seek for shelter second, in order to survive. Entertainment, luxury goods and all other types of fancy items come after the fact that you have found food and shelter to live comfortable and survive.

Robert Kiyosaki, the author of the book "Rich Dad, Poor Dad" says that if you want to become a millionaire, you have to become an entrepreneur, a business owner or an investor. You can do, all of those three at the same time. In the massive scale of business, those who are professional real estate experts, make a business out of every real estate purchase they make, by creating a Limited Liability Company, or a Corporation, to manage their property. They do so, not only because it limits their liability as individuals, but also because they get some tax incentives out of this process. The truth is that if you want to become a millionaire, you have to begin by building your own businesses first. In the real estate context, you can make a business out of every purchase you make, to save your self from personal liabilities. Therefore, begin to think about nurturing and growing your real estate portfolio. If you do it correctly, it can turn you into a millionaire, or a billionaire, if you want.

Also, as Kevin O'Laery from "Shark Tank" says, 'Never own a position that does not return capital." Meaning in the Real Estate context, never own a piece of property that does not offer you a return of investment. And remember, once you understand, or have developed a system to build or create wealth through Real Estate, all you have to do is to scale it up, replicate it, amplify it and train and hire others to further expand your business and millions of dollars if you wish.

Real estate Wholesaling

Before we move into the next chapter, let's talk a little about the wholesaling process in real estate. Wholesaling is indeed a very good mechanism to make money in real estate. "It is similar to flipping, except that the time frame is much shorter and no repairs are made to the home. As the wholesaler never actually purchases a home, real estate wholesaling is much less risky than flipping, which can involve renovation costs and carrying costs. Real estate wholesaling also involves much less capital than flipping. Generally speaking earnest money payments on a few properties is sufficient. Success depends on the wholesaler's knowledge of the market and connection to investors for quick sales". (Segal, 2018)

"To put it simply, wholesaling in real estate occurs when a property is available to be bought for less than it's worth—often because it's in bad condition or because the seller is motivated to drop their price. Your job is to get it under contract at that "wholesale" price. Then, you sell it "as-is" for a little bit more to a cash buyer, who makes a substantial profit when they resell it again someday, or by keeping it in their portfolio as a rental property. How do you make money? Simple...you make the difference between the contract price (between you and seller) and what your buyer agrees to pay for it. This usually means $3,000-$10,000 or more"(Rehabvaluator.com, 2018). A very important element to wholesaling is "to add a contingency to the purchase contract that allows the wholesaler to back out of the deal if he is unable to find a buyer before the expected closing date. This limits the wholesaler's risk". (Segal, 2018)

Chapter 2

Master the Art of Selling

There is this wrongful, bad stigma about salespeople around the world. My take is that this wrongful stigma was created because a lot of people were not trained to understand the sales process correctly, but also because a lot of people had a bad experience with a lousy salesperson at some point in the past. And I understand that. We all want to avoid bad experiences. The sad truth is that every industry, every country, and every culture, has good people and bad people. And that is also true, for the sales industry.

But the reality is that the sales process is part of the day-to-day activities of every human being. Whether if you are a kid who wants to sell their parents the idea that you are good students by conducting all the home-works on time, so that you can get to play videogames all night afterwards, or whether if you are the parent who wants to sell the idea to their kids that the "Spinach Soup" is good for them, so that they can grow up to be rich, famous and intelligent. The reality is that everybody, or nearly every human being with full health, intellect, and capacities, is a salesperson, whether if they want to admit it or not, everybody sells something nearly every day of their lives.

The truth is that we all sell and we all buy, every day of our lives. This is part of our daily routines. Some of us buy more than what we sell, and some of us sell more than what we buy. Those who sell more than what they buy, of course, make a lot more money and obtain a more significant financial benefit from this activity, than those who are always on the buying side, spending. Therefore, if you really want to be rich, or you want to maintain and grow your capital and wealth for the long and short term, you have to master the art of selling. By the way, if you have already mastered the art of selling, you already deserve the status of being a millionaire, or a billionaire.

The truth is that if you have mastered the art of selling, you are on your way to make a lot of money because if that is the case, you have mastered one of those very important attributes that are considered as *Money Making* skills. And this attribute goes hand-to-hand, with the principle of arbitrage, which again, means to *buy low and sell high.*

According to Dan Lok, a Canadian Self Made Millionaire and book author who has made a lot of millions, but also has made a big impact in a lot of people's lives from around the world, one of the most important money making skills, among others, includes the ability to *close a sale.* But in order for you to develop that skill to full capacity, you have to destroy the notion first, that selling is a bad thing. In fact, on the other hand, you have to be able to understand, digest, embrace and make it clear in your mind the idea *that selling is a good thing.* But for that mindset shift to develop in your head, you have to make sure that you sell quality products that people need and are willing to buy, no matter what. Make sure that you are selling products and services that are solving a problem for your customers and making them loyal to you and your products. Meaning, selling products that provide value to the market place, not the opposite. Let me remind you that a happy customer is a loyal customer, but also, it's a customer that will bring you more clients or customers via the referral system and the mouth-to-mouth, marketing effect, which continues to be the most effective marketing strategy that exists in the market place.

Let's conduct a quick exercise to begin the process of changing our mindset when it comes to selling. Please, go outside of your reading room for a brief moment and repeat the following mantra:

Selling is Good!!

Selling feels so good!!

Selling is Healthy!!

Selling is Sexy!!

Go ahead and repeat that mantra for a couple of times. More than ten times every day if you can. Make sure you repeat this mantra until this message sinks into your mind, your heart, your body, and your soul. Repeat that process as many times as you want, or need, until the proper abundant selling mindset becomes part of your life and lifestyle, forever.

Especially because; selling is a good thing whether if you want to believe it or not. Especially when you are offering quality products and services that provide a solution for your customers and makes them happy and satisfied. Let me correct that, especially, if your customers or clients keep coming for more and are happy and satisfied.

Imagine Steve Jobs and his Apple products for example. Most of the people in the world, loved his Apple products, as they were rapidly becoming loyal and happy customers without hesitation. The truth is that Steve Job's customers always wanted to come back for more Apple products, no matter what, while at the same time, showing their newly purchased products to their family and friends via the use of the powerful word of mouth. That was definitely the perfect sales scenario that every company envied from the Apple Company during the Steve Job years. That type of scenario where the entire world was willing to die so that they could obtain the latest Apple products, services or technology so that they could brag about it to the entire world.

Down to the core, Steve Jobs loved and believed in the sales process. He probably loved the sales process more than the research and development process of his company, because it was during the sales process, only then, when Steve Jobs obtained his rewards, which were: **money, cash, success, and global recognition.** Of course, all the Apple products were a phenomenon during Steve Job's era, and most of them were offering tremendous value to their customers via the means of a great design, innovation and a beautiful easy to use integrating technology. So much value, that nearly all of Apple customers during the Steve Jobs era had become loyal customers of all the Apple products and services; to include the Apple Music store. Imagine that.

The truth is that if you really want to become a millionaire, or if you are already a Millionaire or a Billionaire, just like Steve

Jobs was, you know that selling is good. Chances are, that effectively knowing the art of selling is what made you a millionaire or billionaire in the first place. And since everyone in this world, to a certain extent, is a salesperson as we mentioned before, you might as well embrace it to full capacity. In fact, you have got to love the art of selling.

Especially if you are not a millionaire; if you want to become a millionaire, you have to embrace the sales process to the point where you can scale up the selling of your products and services to the masses, or the largest amount of people as possible. Don't forget that the second principle of wealth creation is the scalability principle, which means, take your one product or service, and sell it to the masses.

Go ahead and repeat the following mantra or motto once again, for a couple of times in order for you to ratify, that you are, and you love being a salesperson.

What do I do? I Sell
What do we do? We sell.
What Do I do? I love to sell!!
What do I want to do? I want to sell to the masses.

Quick note: If you are already a millionaire, you already love the sales process. And if you want to become a millionaire, you have got to understand, that mastering and loving the sales process, is what is going to get you there. But also, you have to embrace this process as part of your soul. You have to make it a lifestyle, on a daily basis. Take the sales process, and tattoo it in your bones as your life's love.

Direct Sales vs. Indirect Sales

There are two different types of sales processes. There is a direct sales process, and there is an indirect sales process. The big difference between them is that the direct sales process requires direct personal communication with your customer, where through the process of influence and persuasion, you facilitate the purchase of an item, product, or service to your client. When I say influence and persuasion, I mean it in a positive way. Chances are; your product or service is going to offer your customer a good solution to a problem; so you have to always believe in your self and the products and services you are selling, before deciding to sell any product in the market place. The direct selling process, it's also known as a business to customer (B2C) transaction, due to the fact, that during this process, your company sells directly to the customer without the help of any external forces.

In the indirect sales process, on the other hand, a company uses a middle person, or another middle company, as the facilitator to make the selling of your products and services. This form of selling is also known as a Business-to-Business (B2B) process, because "Company A" makes a deal with "Company B," to distribute and sell "Company's A" products and services to the end consumer. Meaning, other company or commissioned independent sales agent, will sell and distribute "Company's A" products and services to the world.

Let's think of the "Best Buy" store, for instance, one of the leading retail consumer electronic stores across the United States. Best Buy, for example, serves as the middleman, or the physical and online distributor, for hundreds of thousands of companies that use the Best Buy Store to sell their products and services to their customers. Best Buy is an excellent example of an indirect distribution sales channel that is very effective and popular across the United States. Companies like Sony, Apple, Canon, Nikon, and many others, sell their product and services to their consumers, via the physical or online Best Buy stores. This retail chain store brand carries a lot of good reputation and accessibility to the U.S consumer, in nearly every city across the United States of America.

By the way, you can apply both, the direct and indirect sales channels to all of your products and services, at all times. Remember, that the more channels you open to sell your products or services, the more chances you will get of making a sale. It is also vital to keep the principle of scalability in your mind at all times during the entire sales strategy creation process. Don't forget that one sale is not going to make you a millionaire, but thousands or millions of sales will. Always consider the idea of selling your products and services, at a scalable rate, where you can sell, to thousands of people at the same point in time. For those purposes, you will need to have a good marketing and advertisement strategy that will give you the greatest amount of exposure of your brands and products to the world. But we'll talk more about marketing and advertisement strategies in greater detail ahead.

The Direct Sales Process:

The direct sales process requires multiple different methods that include Face-to-Face selling, Door-to-Door Selling, Cold Calling, Party Plan selling, and Email selling. "You can phone the customer, see them Face-to-Face or even use email. The communication link between the company and the prospective customer is direct" (Lynda Banks, 2018)[4].

"Some of the most common types of direct sales are those that involve you selling over the counter to your customer, through direct mail marketing or selling on your own website"[5]. Let me remind you that when a consumer visits your store, the chances are that there is a 50% chance that he or she will make a purchase in your store because they are already in buying mode, but also, they are looking for a specific product in your store. If you have that product available for them, at the right price, with the proper customer service, you will make that sale.

In the direct sales process, you are in charge of the sales communication process of the company yourself. Therefore, you have to develop a "Go Getter" strategy that could be quite intimidating to a few people, because you are going to take the initiative of talking directly to the customer, instead of the customer coming and looking for you. There is a big difference when the consumer comes to you, looking for a product or service than when you go to the consumer disrupting their time and attention. A few people may perceive it as an aggressive sales strategy, that aims to look, search, find and close the sale process right on the spot. But if you have sharpened those direct selling skills, or if you have a team of professional sales agent with direct sales closing skills, you will be opening a lot of good business and sales opportunities for your company. Remember, going back to Steve Jobs. He used to say the following: "some people don't know they need your product until you presented to them," so the direct sales process in a way, is a method for you to present your product or service to those people who did not know about the possible solution you are offering them. Also remember, if you don't know whether if a prospect, client or customer may need your service, well, then simply ask. Asking when you have a question is a great attribute, mastered by those outgoing individuals with excellent communication skills. If you have those skills, or you have a team of professionals who possess those types of skills, then you are ahead of the game.

For those reasons, a good direct sales plan includes a lead generation strategy, also known as a prospecting strategy, where you'll be able to identify your specific target market, or niche, or group of consumers. Chances are they all share unique characteristics that can help you identify them as a robust set of consumers for your products or services. You can determine your target market or niche consumer group based on the unique characteristics of the products you sell.

For example, if you want to sell "Fishing Bait" in the area of San Francisco Bay, you will have to conduct market research that will tell you the characteristics of the fishing crews and consumers in the San Francisco Bay area. Let's say that your research shows you that most of the fishers in the area of San Francisco Bay are males, from the ages of 20 to 60, who love outdoors and like to buy boats. Also, they usually attend boat shows and water outdoor sporting events.

Right after you get this information, you find out that there is a boat show coming in a few weeks. You sign up for a sales tent in the event, and you begin to do your direct selling process at this event, but also the prospecting and the lead generation process that you need at the same time. All eventual prospect customers who are interested in your products and services will approach your tent, to see what you have to offer. If you do not make a direct sale right on the spot, you can get their information, and begin the process of building a business to customer relationship with them. Chances are, you did not have the unique color of bait that they were looking for at your sales tent, but you have the color they are looking for at your store. Therefore, if you can't sell your products on your sales tent right away, you can sell them later on, via an online sales channel or by having your prospects visiting your store. In that sense, by the process, of asking your prospects for their email and contact information, you can begin to develop a good customer relationship with your prospective client that could give you a continuous return of investment in the future by the means of future sales.

Don't forget that after one customer makes a purchase, it is essential to try to develop a good relationship with the customer, so that they can become your loyal customers. Remember that a happy customer is a customer that comes back, but also, it can bring additional customers to your store.

Let's say that John, for example, just bought a $50.00 dollars, all-weather terrain Parka Jacket from your store and that he is a happy customer. The chances are that John will come back later on for the pants, the boots, and the all-terrain weather hat when he gets a chance. Also, he will probably begin to buy the bait from you, on a weekly basis, as he prepares to go fishing every weekend on his boat. Therefore, an initial $50.00 US dollar sale just augmented into a $250.00 purchase, with the ability to grow even to an even higher value over the years. Let's also say that John also brought to you two more clients that wanted to purchase the same Jacket. That is an additional $100.00 from a happy customer. Let's say that the new customers, John brought with him, are also happy, and they buy more products for themselves, but also bring the other two customers. Well, you just created a sales chain event that started just with one excellent customer service activity and the excellent relationship practice that you developed with John in the first place. So never underestimate the increasingly high return of investment that good customer service can provide you.

We can also talk about the "Up Sale" opportunity that is created once a customer makes their first purchase in your store, because when John, bought his first jacket, you could have also offered him a new fishing net that you have in promotion, or even, a new fishing boat, that you may have available in your store. The possibilities are endless when it comes to the **"Up Selling strategy**," once a customer has made their first purchase in your store. But, we'll talk more about Up Selling later on in this chapter.

One quick tip, when it comes to selling, is that higher value items, or high ticket sales, will nearly always give you greater economic benefit over mass production selling, not only because when prices are higher, the return of investment might be higher, but also because, in the direct sales channel, higher ticket sales, will always give you a greater incentive to make the phone call, or make a direct sale, than selling 10 pens in the market place. If you sell a boat, that the manufacturer sold you at a $12,000.00 USD price, for $18,000.00, you would have made a $6,000 profit in one transaction. 10 pens that you bought at $1, and sell at $2, on the other hand, will only give you a 10.00 dollars profit. So if you want to become a millionaire, focus on the higher priced products and services, rather than the low-profit-margin making products, like a pen. Unless you own a Pen manufacturer Company and sell pens to the masses; then, you will have a completely different story. But always try to focus on high-ticket sales, rather than low-ticket sales.

If you are a millionaire, your consulting services can also be valued at a very high price. Some expert millionaires entrepreneurs, also sell their consulting time at an incredibly high price rate. If you are a Millionaire or a Billionaire, think about how much an hour from your life costs, and sell it in the market place. This is also another good way, or strategy to make additional income or money via the high ticket consulting services.

Indirect Sales:

Indirect sales are those that are conducted through affiliates or a reseller. Two examples are Avon, Herbalife or any product you purchase at the local grocery store. Basically, it means that other independent sales associates or retail stores sell the products for you. Remember, the more channels for the sales process you have, the better. Of course, if there is a good return on investment. Let's not forget that everything in business also carries a cost, so if the cost of putting your products for sale in other stores exceeds the revenue, then, I do not recommend you to use this method. After all, principle number 3 of this book is the following: to **"Keep Your Cost Down".** And that goes for every operation transaction you conduct from your wealth portfolio. But we'll go deep into that topic, more in detail, in the next chapter.

The indirect sales process is an excellent method for selling to the masses because the indirect method uses retail stores that are well known and are already selling to the masses. Let's think about the Walmart, Target, Best Buy, and Tiger Direct stores. These are all well-known retail stores that sell a large number of different products, to include electronic products across the United States. Companies like Microsoft, Sony, Panasonic, Nikon, and Canon, use these retail stores as an indirect sales channel that allows the consumer to obtain their products at their local stores. Let us not forget, that brands like Microsoft, Sony, Panasonic, Nikon, and Canon, do not have Retail Stores across most of the cities of the U.S, just like Apple does, so these companies have to rely on indirect sales channels to sell their products to their consumers in the first place. Of course, companies like Walmart and Best Buy win by selling these Sony's or Microsoft products at a slightly higher ticket price, but they also get a commission out of every sale they make. So, it is a win-win scenario for both, the retail and the manufacturing company. That is if the deal was conducted right, by effectively favoring both companies.

Another indirect sales channels could be used via some of the most popular e-commerce channels. E-commerce retail platforms like Amazon.com, for example, are also considered as an indirect sales channel because they offer products from other companies via their exclusive e-commerce platform. Although if you create your own store in the Amazon platform, it becomes a direct sales channel, because you would be managing your own online Amazon store, and therefore, you will be selling your own products. All you'll have to do is just paying a percentage fee of every transaction the Amazon website charges, for the use of their platform. The truth is that the more exposure and the more channels your products are being sold in, the better. So try to have your products in your online store, your physical stores, and all the indirect sales retail stores.

Sharpening you Selling Techniques

The process of sharpening your selling skills should be one of your life mandates. Because at the end, it does not matter how good your product is, if you cannot sell it to the world, you are not providing any value to the market place.

Sales skills are an essential part of the business world, if not one of the most important parts of it. Because at the end; the sales activity is considered as the most important lead generating process that exists in every industry, in order to create and obtain revenue. Without revenue, and more importantly net income, your company would not be able to survive.

Another critical element of sharpening your sales techniques, include developing the leadership and motivational skill that would allow you to lead a group of sales sharks, or wolves, who could sale your products and services for you. One of the most important characteristics of a great sales leader includes discipline, initiative, confidence, resilience, leadership, motivational skills, and pulse.

Remember that when you decide to become a millionaire, you will always have to be in persuasive mode at all times, trying to influence every decision or action in your favor, and that is the truth for everyone. But you will mostly need to have sales leadership skills because, by the time you are a millionaire, you will have to hire as many sales experts as you can, who will be working for you. Because at the end, when it comes to economies of scale and leading sales teams, you will have to live and act in leadership and persuasive mode constantly, in order to achieve the sales goals for the day, the week, the month and the year. When you become a millionaire, or if you become a millionaire, you will continuously be, selling ideas, goods, services, to others, so that you can make the revenue you need to keep your business moving forward.

Also, always remember that it is better to lead a group of sales experts and consultants than to be a sales consultant yourself. Of course, you have to know the sales consultancy process, and experience how it works, so that you know what it means. But as a sales consultant, you will be paid a commission for each product that you sell. However, if you lead a team of sales people, you will be getting a commission out of every sale, one of your consultants make. If you have a team of 10 sales consultants, and each one of them makes a sale on a given day, you will be getting a commission out of every one of them. In all of these direct selling cases, whether if you are the lead sales manager, or the sales consultant, the main skill that you will have to master or develop, is the ability to effectively close the sale.

UPSALES

Whether if your company size is small or large, your company needs to build or have a robust, successful and expandable sales strategy. Because a proper sales strategy, if planned and executed correctly, is going to give your company the revenue and income it needs to grow and become successful. It does not matter, what kind of industry or sector your private company operates in. If your company has an effective sales strategy, your company will be successful.

Of course, a good sales strategy cannot be implemented without a good "Up Sale" tactic. The *"Up Sale tactic"* should be incorporated into every sales strategy on a daily basis, because multiple studies have shown, that once a customer makes a purchase at any given store, the sale of a second item, comes very easy, almost automatically for the customer, in some cases.

An excellent example to showcase this tactic is the one used by all the Mac Donald's restaurants. All the selling associates within the Mac Donald's restaurants will always ask their customers the following questions; "Would you like fries with that? Or, would you like to make it a combo? Nearly 95% of all consumers will say "yes." And that is simply the art of *"Up-Selling"* to the core.

Let's say that you go to buy a motorcycle in your favorite motorcycle store. Let' say that you saw the motorcycle of your dreams, and you bought it. Immediately right after, the sales associate will ask you, would you like to buy a helmet or the Jacket, Boots, and Gloves that you need for your protection? If you say yes, well, you have just been a victim of the upselling process. But these are all items that the buyer had not accounted for, in the first place. The idea is that after every purchase, you can always sell something else to the customer, and this system goes for every industry. The salesperson, in this case, can even sale a maintenance package to the client, since the maintenance process will be a requirement for the long term care of the motorcycle.

Let me give you a quick example from a funny experience I had the other day at the mall. The truth is that other day, I went into the mall, without even thinking of buying any product. I have to be honest; I use the "buy low, sell high" technique almost everywhere I go, every time I can. But at the mall, you will always get higher ticket prices, than when you buy from an outlet or a manufacturing store. However, as I was waiting for one person, I entered one store just to browse a little. I ended up, loving one shirt. I tried it, loved how it looked on me and took it to the counter. Right before paying for the shirt, I entered into the suit department section of the store, without even realizing. As I kept waiting for this person, I tried two suits that grabbed my attention and took them to the counter. The funny story is that by the time I got to the counter, I had also picked up a few sets of business ties, and a few leather belts. Without even thinking about it, I had ended up spending a few thousand dollars, in a few items that I did not need before walking into the mall. Just because of one initial Shirt that I loved.

Another common practice that is continuously used to accelerate, or incentivize the closing of a sale, is the use of the "Urgency" tactic during the closing period of the sale. This goes hand-to-hand with the promotional attributes of the item you are selling. With the "Urgency Tactic" or methodology, you offer the customer a "Fear of Missing Out" scenario, by giving them a deadline in the buying process, where if they don't buy up to a certain deadline, they will lose all the promotional value that its offered to them.

For example, a 50% promotional sign was placed in the shirt that I loved triggered my purchase, in the first place. But in order to get that promo, I had to buy that shirt the same day I walked into the store. Otherwise, I would have lost the promotion. Since I thought it was a good deal, I decided to buy the shirt. Little did I know, that I was going to buy two suits, and a couple of business ties and a few leather belts right after in the same store.

We'll go more in detail into this "Urgency tactic" in the future, and how it's used, once we enter into the "Marketing Like a Millionaire" chapter, where you will be able to obtain the latest tactics and techniques available in the marketing discipline for closing or converting marketing and advertisement strategies into real sales.

Also remember, when selling, it is essential that you understand people's pain points, and try to solve them effectively with your products or services. What are the drivers that push your customers to buy your products? Is it that they want to look good? Is it that they need better transportation? Is it that they cannot watch their favorite baseball games live because of work? Whatever type of pain point, you are trying to solve for your customer, remember that the solution you provide must provide relief to the pain of your customer. Your product should be able to solve your customer's problem and via the method of solving a problem, using excellent customer service and developing brand loyalty from your customers in return.

Chapter 3

Keep Your Cost Low

I know. Probably a lot of you reading this book thought of me being kind of a stingy person, from reading the example I gave you about my mall experience at the end of chapter 2 and the "up sale" process that happens nearly in every sales transaction in the market place. The truth is that, as time moves forward, I have become a little more conservative about how I spend my money, kind of like Jeff Bezos. The truth is that I spend little money on things that I don't need, and spend a lot of money on all the businesses that I have. In a strange way, business management has become my life, and I do not invest in anything unless I see a return on investment. Somehow, at some point in my life, I realized that all my expensive cars and motorcycles, were not really a necessity, but they were all similar to a childish dream, that I had kept during my early years when I was young and furious. And I am not saying this to discourage you. I am not telling you that buying all these expensive items is bad. I am just saying that if they do not offer a good return on investment for me in whatever shape or form, then I do not buy them, and neither should you.

The fact is that part of any business success is to bring a *"Profit"* to your business. And a profit means, " _the money a business makes after accounting for all expenses_." The key words here are "after accounting for all expenses." *Revenue,* on the other hand, is, the total amount of money the business receives from its customers for its products and services *without* accounting for any operating expenses. The key words here are, "without accounting for all expenses." A profit is also known as a *"Net income*," which is very different from a company's revenue. And you will need to have a positive *net income,* in order to be successful in your company's operations.

The reality is that the real success of a company is only measured by the *"Net Income"* of the company. Not the revenue, because the *"Net Income*," is equal to the total sales of your company, minus the cost of goods sold, minus selling and administrative expenses, minus taxes and minus other interest expenses.

So, if your *"Company A"* makes USD 3,000,000.00 of total sales during the year 2019, but it spends USD 2,950.000.00 in operating expenses to make that revenue, then, your "Company A" made a **"Net Profit"** of USD 50,000.00 for the year.

And if your *"Company B"* made USD 6,540,000.00 in revenue, but it spends $7,000,000.00 in operating expenses to make that revenue, then your company is operating at a net loss of USD 460,000.00 for the same year. There will be no profit in this scenario. There is a loss instead.

In the massive scale of business, all major operating cost does matter, that is why, it is vital for you to develop a mindset, or lifestyle, of reducing cost in as many things as possible within your business, so that your company can make a *big profit.*

Think of Warren Buffett and Jeff Bezos for example. Two very successful billionaires dollar Investors who can buy any companies in the market place, like they buy candy from the candy store. Warren Buffett worth is about 75 to 82 Billion dollars in 2019, and Jeff Bezos is worth about between 135 and 143 Billion dollars. I give you approximate numbers, mainly because these numbers are fluctuating on a weekly basis, and different reports offer different sets of numbers depending on the agency.

The truth is that these people are billionaires and they live a very calm life, with very austere lifestyles. They both like to drive small, simple cars, and wear simple clothes, instead of extravagant clothing. They like to make money of course in the billion dollar numbers, but they have developed this buy low sell high mentality, that encourages them to keep the cost down in all cases. Not only within their businesses but also, within their lifestyles. I would like to think that they serve as a great example of humility and hard work for their employees, but also to the world itself, because they are also **"Self Made Billionaires"**, who by means of hard work and adequately investing their time, efforts and money into risky and innovative profitable endeavors, they were able to capitalize in large numbers over the long term. Who would not like or want to have the amount of money these two boys have across their business portfolios, I think everyone would.

Answer the following question:

Is it better for you to have 10,000,000,00 Million dollars in your bank account, or is it better for you to have 9,000.000.00 dollars in your bank account. Which number do you prefer?

I would like to think that you'd rather have 10 million, rather than 9 million dollars in your bank account. And for those purposes, is good to apply the principle number three of this book, which is to *"keep your operational cost low."* This is very important.

Principle # 3

Keep Your Cost Low

Of course, there are some cases where the austerity approach might not be so good or exciting; depending on the type of business model your company carries. But also on the type of niche or target market, your company works with. Within the wealth creation market, for example, there is a serious segment of the market that is driven by the opportunity of one day, people being able to live the millionaire lifestyle, full of luxury goods, boats, private planes, Ferrari's, private islands, and hopefully a Rolls Royce, along the way. And that is good as well. Everyone's life goals are different, and everyone should do with their life as they wish, as well as with their money.

There are a few good mentors that I have; who genuinely love their Roll Royce cars, and everyone around them admires them and admires their cars, including myself. The fact is that some luxury items are indeed attention grabbers, and if you use them correctly, they could bring a lot of value to your business. Take a look a Grant Cardone or Dan Lok for example, two self-made millionaires who use their Rolls Royce cars, to grab everyone's attention via their Youtube.com channels and other social media platforms to drive traffic to their businesses, but also to let everyone know that they are self-made millionaires. Of course, those beautiful Rolls Royce cars do also serve them as a good publicity tactic that drives them a lot of traffic to all of their businesses online.

Let us not forget, however, that even though Grant Cardone and Dan Lok, have a pretty diversified wealth portfolio that includes Real Estate and other investment forms, they also are great marketers and salespeople, who make millions of dollars via their digital platforms and online sales channels. And they all begin with a simple attention grabber video, such as a video of them inside a Rolls Royce *"ad"* that is offered via all social media and youtube.com channels towards a specific target market in the form of paid advertisement. A lot of people will click on that *ad*. These millionaires make millions of dollars out of the youtube.com, Facebook or Instagram *"advertisement"* programs. With one simple social media *ad*, they instantly get credibility as millionaires via the Youtube.com and social media channels. They also get thousands of followers, leads and prospective customers to visit their online stores where they will convert those visits, or online traffic into sales. It all begins with one simple Rolls Royce *"video ad'* that was placed on someone's social media feed. The truth is there are people today, making millions and millions of dollars, via the use of proper digital advertisement and marketing techniques.

Once you click on their ad, they'll send you directly to an online landing page, where they will get you to buy some of their books, consulting services, their millionaire training and webinars programs or courses, and other digital and non-digital services and products that they are offering online.

So, in both cases their Rolls Royce's are essentially the hook they use, to grab people's attention and have them listening to them. Think of them, as the Superbowl advertisement hook, in the Youtube.com sphere, where a Rolls Royce is what everyone, would like to have. Every time they post a video on their Youtube.com channels with these cars, people's attention is grabbed, because people from all backgrounds in life, know what a Rolls Royce means to them, but also, nearly everybody from every corner of the world wants to become a millionaire. So what better to showcase this self-made millionaire stories, via the use of lavish luxury items and mansions. Hell, not to mention, Grant Cardone, just bought his first private jet, simply to showcase, how massive his wealth portfolio is. And people love these types of stories, and so does Grand Cardone. The Private jets and the Rolls Royce's is what gives Grant Cardone his credibility and makes people believe him and his messages. But we'll go more into detail, into the digital marketing and advertisement channels, once we enter our chapter 4, which is titled "Marketing and Advertising like a Millionaire."

Of course, there is a "keep your cost low strategy" on every advertisement plan that you develop, because, even when it comes to your advertisement budget, there are ways to get more for your money, than what you paid for. For now, let's focus on keeping your operation cost low so that your company can make a profit, instead of only revenue.

The fact is that there are multiple stories of people, who have become millionaires, and then, by the whisper of the wind, they have found themselves, filing for Bankruptcy a few years later; becoming poor again, like they used to be before. People like Mike Tyson, Pamela Anderson, and MC Hammer, wasted, or did not properly handled the money they had to create more wealth, but instead, they wasted it all, by having a lifestyle that was lavish and wasteful.

These are seriously successful athletes and actors who had no idea about how to manage their wealth and ended up spending all of their money and economic resources, in things that did not offer them any return of investment. In other words, they did not know how to maintain or grow their wealth. It appears that the only thing they thought about when they became wealthy, was to spend, spend, and spend, and that is not a good way of staying millionaire over the long term.

For those reasons, *saving* is also a good strategy and attribute of the wealth creation process. You have to understand that money is leverage, and the more money you have, the more leverage you will have in the world. That is why, we always repeat the motto that says, "It is always wiser, smarter and sexier, to make more money, rather than spending it." Otherwise, you will be operating at a loss, in every business cycle over the future, and may lose all your wealth in the process.

For those reasons, is better to focus more in having a positive net income when you have a business, and keeping your operational cost low, because at the end, It is best, to negotiate from a position of power, and money equals to power and leverage in today's world. Be jealous with your money. Better yet, be stingy with it.

Chapter 4

Marketing and Advertising like a Millionaire.

Marketing and Advertisement like a Millionaire Principle # 4

If you really want to make big money and scale up the selling of your products and service to the masses, this process requires from you to have a solid, intelligent and diverse marketing and advertisement strategy, that will allow you to get customers to buy your products and services in the first place. It does not matter how many products or services you have. It does not matter, whether if you have produced the latest I-phone 20X, with 5G Capability and a 24 Mega Pixel camera built in. The truth is that if you do not know how to properly advertise, or market your product, you are not going to make even one sale anywhere, no matter what.

The reality is that *sales revenue* goes hand-to-hand with marketing and advertisement spending. You cannot sell any product to the world if you cannot present it to the eyes of the people who could be interested in your products and services in the first place. For those reasons, the first element of a good marketing and advertisement strategy includes identifying *your niche segment or your target market.*

Niche-focused

A few years back, while I was wondering behind the scenes at the New York Fashion Show, a good friend of mine introduced me to one of the top Fashion Business professors at the New York University. After exchanging a few words with some other film producers from the same event, I asked him, what is the one secret, or piece of advice you would give me if I wanted to succeed in the business and marketing world? He told me, if you want success in any kind of business, you have got *to find your niche.*

" A *niche market* is a focused, targetable portion of a market. By definition, then, a business that focuses on a niche is addressing a need for a product or service that is not being addressed by mainstream providers. Establishing a niche market allows you to provide products and services to a group that other businesses have overlooked" (Susan Ward, 2018([5].

A good example would be the luxury cars, or luxury boats niche market. There is a very exclusive, affluent, millionaire or billionaire clientele who would like or love to invest in buying these kinds of products. These are more like lifestyle products that people use to showcase their economic status, but there is also a segment of this market, that uses all these products and services as a business model, by renting or booking parties in their boats and making a significant profit from it. I've seen this a lot, happening in the city of Miami.

The reality is that these are also high maintenance items, that would also allow you to offer a whole variety of sub-products, or services, designed to maintain and sustain these kinds of products in top conditions. Therefore, you can definitely use the "*Up sale*" technique in this case, that I explained to you earlier in this book.

In that sense, a Niche market is also similar to a target market, or market segment, that has very unique and consistent attributes and identifiable behaviors attached to its customers. One of the greatest business assets you will obtain by adequately identifying your niche market; is that you will develop a clear understanding of **who your consumers are,** and what are the demographic and psychographic characteristics they possess. Let's say again, that you are selling boats, or Yates in the city if Miami. Well, you are not going to sell them to single moms, who have two jobs and three kids, who are struggling to put food on their table.

The reality is that if you really want these boats to be sold quickly, you have got to first identify the attributes and unique characteristics of your prospect customers, or your target market. The buyer persona, or **personal attributes**, demographics, and psychographics of the people who would be interested in buying these types of luxury transportation products. In this case, your target market would be the affluent, wealthy, White, Latinos or Black males, who love to go out fishing. They also love Sunday boat trips with their families and friends. Or they are just business people, who are making successful businesses revenue from their fishing and open seas tourism operations. You can also target, the affluent, rich males, who just retired from a cold city, who would like to live near a lake or the ocean in a warm place. They can even live in the city of Chicago if they please, a city that has some amazing lakes within their periphery, but it also houses the third largest population of billionaires in the world. Therefore identifying your **target market** is the first, most important thing you will have to do if you want to have a successful marketing and advertisement strategy in your business.

The second thing that you will need to develop if you want to sell your products and services more effectively is to create a **marketing plan**, that will allow you to identify the **consumer behavior** of your target market. Things like, what programs they are watching? What type of events do they attend? Where do they network and gather? Do they use social media? How often do they use it? What is the best way to reach to them?

This type of information or business intelligence is called **Marketing analytics**, and these are very useful tools, to understand the overall consumer behavior patterns of the people buying your products.

Within the online e-commerce business model, for example, there are some very powerful analytics tools that are offered by companies such as Google and Facebook, but also by Youtube.com. By the way, let me remind you that Google owns Youtube.com if you did not know.

The bottom line is that when it comes to digital marketing; the analytic tools these types of companies provide are simply amazing. They will help you to optimize your company's online workflow and revenue, by letting you know exactly how your consumers are behaving in relationship with your products. In that sense, a good marketing and advertisement plan should implement a good set of **analytic tools** as a priority, when it comes to creating or developing an effective marketing plan.

Another key element within the marketing and advertisement world, especially when it comes to digital marketing, is the use of the **Search Engine Optimization** or (SEO). The *SEO* tool facilitates the process of how your customers find your websites, during their own personal searches online. There is an inbound and an outbound component when it comes to digital marketing. During the inbound process, *the customers search for you*. In the outbound process, *you search for the customers*. For those reasons, companies like Google have developed these mechanisms of facilitating the process of how your customer can find you, in very effective ways. Via the use of a tool called **Search Engine Optimization, or SEO**, companies like Google, Bing, and Yahoo, can help your customers find your company online more easily and effectively when you pay for a Google search ad, or a Bing search ad, or a Yahoo search ad. When you pay for an advertisement within the Google search engine, which is the most popular search engine from around the world, chances are you will be driving a lot more business and online traffic to your website and your other online platforms. This goes for **Google, Bing, Yahoo** or any other type of search engine platform that exists in the World Wide Web.

If you optimize your online website store for the *SEO* process, you will become more competitive online, and you will be able to drive more traffic to your website and convert that traffic into sales. Of course, you will have to offer the proper set of promotional incentives and facilitate the process of making a purchase to your clients when they arrive at your website if you truly want to make that sale. It is even very useful nowadays, to have a very concise or precise "*pay and close, landing page*" when your customers arrive to your website, so that they can make a purchase, or book your service fast, without having them wondering too much around your website, but instead, taking them directly into the landing closing page where you make the sale. Remember, people don't go to your website, just because they are wondering around.

They go to your website because they need your product or service, so you have to make the process of them buying from you, *fast and easy.* For those reasons, we'll go more into detail, into how to properly set up of a landing page in a few paragraphs ahead. There are companies like Exur.com, or salesforce.com, or mailchimp.com; who are experts in the creation of landing pages. I recommend that you visit these websites for those purposes.

Within the Search Engine Optimization strategy, however, there are two ways to optimize your online stores. Search engine optimization is a process that can be performed *organically* by introducing *keywords* into your website that consumers commonly use to search for their items online. But another mechanism to organically optimize your webpage so that your potential customers can find it more easily online is by writing effective *copywriting* that looks and feels more appealing to your customers than what your competitors use. (*Quick note*: In whatever industry you are, you do not want to compete, if you are already a millionaire, or you want to become a millionaire; what you really must do, in any type of industry you operate, is to try to **dominate the industry.** True visionaries and entrepreneurs are not in any business to compete; they are there to *dominate*).

Back to the SEO process, the second, more effective and pragmatic way of driving traffic to your online business is via the use of **Google ads** service that will put you on top of the search engine pages when people search for products and services related to you online. Let say that you have a *"Boat Rental"* business in the city of Miami and that a group of tourists who are visiting from Canada, are looking forward to renting a boat once they arrive to Miami. The first thing they are going to do when they arrive at the Miami Airport is to type on their Google search engine, *"Boat rental Miami."* If you have the right keywords in your website and if you have paid for the right advertisement via Google ads, you will be appearing on top of the Google list when people look for your services on the Google site. Chances are, that these individuals searching for a boat in Miami will click on your site if you are on top of that Google list.

It is up to you then, now that they have arrived at your page, to guide your prospect customers towards making a purchase. For those reasons, again, having a good *landing page* is essential, so that when customers arrive at your store, they make the *"purchase" right on that page.* I cannot emphasize this enough. A landing page is absolutely necessary for you to convert your online traffic into sales.

The Landing Page

"A *landing page* is a standalone web page, created specifically for the purposes of a marketing or advertising campaign. It's where a visitor *"lands"* when they have clicked on a Google Ad or similar. Landing pages are designed with a single focused objective – known as a *Call to Action (CTA)".* (Unbounce.com, 2019)[6].

A call to action (CTA) is the most important self-described element, within the landing page, delivering only the one single, direct, more effective and persuasive message that you want your consumers to have. These are the *"Buy Now," "Sign Up Now," "Book Now" or "Join our Newsletter Now,"* messages that your consumers will read and follow when they arrive at your page. Whatever type of action you want your consumers to have, you'll have to let them know in your "Call to Action" button or landing page what is it that you want them to do. I cannot emphasize this enough. To be more effective, there should only be one very specific call to action, per landing page. The "*Buy Now*," option is one of the most popular *"Calls to action"* across the World Wide Web, but also across the marketing world.

Landing pages are single pages designed with one only specific purpose, and that is to convert your Google or Facebook ads, into sales. They are also known as **conversion pages**. In the marketing and advertisement world, conversion means, converting your marketing and advertisement campaigns into sales. After all, your marketing and advertisement campaigns would not matter, if you did not convert them into sales. So, therefore, a landing page, with a very unique call to action, is specifically designed to have your customer to take the action that you want them to take. Hopefully, that action will lead you to a sale.

Another beautiful attribute of the landing pages is that they can also be automated. But also, that if you have a clear and solid landing page, this page will give your company the revenue or profit required to grow or maintain; your company's operation and success. When it comes to the digital marketing and advertisement world, the landing page is usually the page that will give you *a happy ending*. In a way, the landing page is the rock star of the digital marketing world.

Classic Vs. Digital Marketing Channels

So, we talked earlier, about the benefits of **keeping your cost down**, when it came to your company's operational expenses. But also, how this process can be even more easily achieved, in the marketing and advertisement industry, by investing most of your budget within all the digital marketing platforms instead of the classical forms of marketing. The truth is that there are many more ways and mechanisms to control, monitor and reach your target audiences, but also meeting your budget needs, inside the digital marketing world, instead of the classical non-digital world. By the way, almost everything nowadays is digital, inside the marketing and advertisement world.

Of course, there is still a lot of value to a TV spot or a TV commercial at peak time in one of the major TV Channels. Or a big street billboard or; a Newspaper *ad* in one of the most influential newspapers in the world. Or even a commercial Radio spot, in one of the most visited radio stations in the world. The truth is that if you ever have the opportunity to participate in any of these high audience mainstream programs, you will be *legitimized* as an influential person, or your company will be legitimized as an influential company, everywhere where that TV spot or commercial radio spot is being delivered.

Magazines, billboards, television programs, news articles, and famous radio spots, are all amazing channels that will grant full *credibility to your message*, or your product and service, wherever that message is being received. So it is good to use these kinds of marketing channels on a regular basis when you can afford them.

But the truth is that with the rise of internet, podcasting, Youtube.com channels, streaming, social media, and direct email marketing, these *digital marketing platforms* have become more effective nowadays, to manage the customer relationship programs of your company, but also to manage how you reach to them on a daily basis, or a weekly basis, more effectively than on a classical marketing channel. Of course, there are still, a lot of people in the world today who look forward to opening up their mailboxes at home, to see the latest marketing messages that are being sent to them via their home mail channels. But the truth is that **email marketing** is considered a lot more useful, and cost-effective, than direct home mail marketing in all cases. The fact is that email marketing is now considered to be **the blood of digital marketing** and it is a lot more effective, traceable and interactive, than regular mail marketing.

The reality is that *"Email marketing"* is the *king* of the marketing kingdom with a 4400% return on investment (ROI) and $44 for every $1 spent. Furthermore, all digital applications such as email marketing can be **automated**. Therefore, by the use of a computer program, you can have those emails delivered to as many people as you want, on a timely basis, without even having to be there writing an email message every single day. The fact is that you can take half of your Sunday to write campaign emails, and program them so that for the next two to three weeks, the emails you wrote that Sunday will be delivered on a timely basis, as you please, in an automated fashion.

The reality is that email marketing is the most effective way of selling your products and services nowadays, because people now check their emails more and more often as part of their daily routines, but also, because if you get to someone's email inbox on a consistent basis, that means they **truly like** your products, services or the type of products that you are offering them.

Of course, you have got to comply with all the laws as well, when it comes to email marketing and reaching to your consumers. The truth is that just like direct phone calls, the customer can request your company not to call them again, or email them again. So the email communication method is much more useful, once it has been determined that the customer is looking for your products, or it has initiated the search of products similar to yours, in the market place. In a way, you have to understand that the email phase of any sales funnel, or marketing conversion funnel, is a *relationship base* phase, close to the end of the sales funnel process, because once you get the email address from a prospect client, that means that they are really interested in purchasing or buying some of your products and services, or building a digital relationship with you.

Several of the most effective digital marketing campaigns that I've seen in the past begins with a very unique promotional ad, where they have people signing up or giving their emails in exchange if they are interested in obtaining your promo. Once you have their email, *the ball is on your side*, and you can deliver to them as many promotions as you want on a constant basis. You can email them all kind of messages, that not only include promotional packages but also thank you notices, your company's newsletters, surveys, loyal customer rewards points, etc. If you happen to have your client's email, you have begun to build a *customer relationship* process with your client, that is difficult to compare via any other marketing channels.

So if you ask me whether if I think that traditional or digital marketing works better? From my experience, I would tell you that digital advertising is more traceable, interactive, and cost-effective. Of course, the traditional marketing channels such as newspapers, television, and radio channels are also effective, and they work well to *legitimize* you as a person, or as a company, wherever their message is being delivered. They have become also part of digital platforms nowadays. For those reasons, I believe that digital marketing is more interactive, precise, measurable, and more affordable. It actually, becomes even more affordable, once you manage to have the email addresses of your customers on a database, especially, if all your clients are happy clients who are loyal to you and your company for the long run.

A good Story Will Always Sell

Because a good story will always sell, especially, if the story is a money making story, it is always good to learn how to *tell a good story*. In a way, the marketing and advertisement industries, are two story-telling industries that are usually used to communicate a product, service or brand message, in a fast, effective and concise way, to the desired target audience.

One of those money making captivating stories includes those of the *self-made millionaires*, who have achieved all their goals by themselves, without the help of anybody else. These are the type of stories that entrepreneurs like Tai Lopez, another successful self-made millionaire, and digital marketer utilize to *drive traffic*, or customers to their websites. What he sells, more than his products and services is his *rags to riches* stories, but also the opportunity to bring everyone on board with him to the millionaire side.

Once you are hooked into his story, by all the extravagance of all his numerous luxury cars and mansions he shows via his youtube.com channel, his Facebook Ads, his Instagram Ads, and other social media advertisement channels, chances are that you'll buy one of his webinars or training courses on *how to make money*. Of course, this is a technique that I also use, so chances are that if you bought this book, you bought it via an online digital platform that placed an ad in your social media or youtube.com stream, and you liked what I offered to you. Keep in mind that I am not discrediting Tai Lopez or Dan Lok, about their online marketing and advertisement tactics. I am just sharing, highlighting, and praising them because these are tactics and stories that *simply work.*

Digital marketing works, and a *good story* will always help you sell your products and services via all the digital and online channels. Because If I try to sell you a regular pen, you will tell me, "I'll give you one dollar for that pen." But If I tell you that the same pen was used by *Martin Luther King* to write his "I have a dream speech," you will pay me a few million dollars for the same pen. In that sense, the only element that I changed when pitching you the pen, *was the story*. And you can see, how *the story* just added a lot of value to the pen. With this simple example, you can see the impact of storytelling in the sales process, but also in nearly every aspect of our lives. The truth is that *stories matter.*

That is why we see nowadays, a very popular *"stories"* section on the Facebook and Instagram mobile applications. Because the reality is that stories, *sell* more than what you think. And just to tell you another piece of information, if you have not noticed it yet, every third or fourth story you see in any of these platforms; will be a paid *ad targeting yourself.* A paid advertisement in your own social media stories section. And *ad* that is targeted to you, because Facebook, which owns Instagram and WhatsApp, *knows* exactly what your online consumer behavior is, just like Google does.

Also, if you pay close attention, you'll see that even in your own newsfeed, at your Facebook or Instagram app, every third or fourth post that you see in there, will be a *targeted ad* made just for you, based on your Google searches and so on. So, yes, you are being *monitored* on your Internet and your online consumer behavior habits, and that is why I told you that all of those Facebook and Google *analytics* tools do work earlier in this chapter. Mostly, because these companies know what, who, when and how you watch or interact with people, products and services online, in every single aspect of your Internet online consumer experience.

For those reasons, I highly recommend for you not to panic about these practices, but instead to **take advantage** of this, new Facebook and Google ads euphoria, and begin to use these platforms as a content producer, or a service provider, or as a business person selling services or a product, or even a brand in these platforms, rather than being simply a consumer. There are a lot of people making millions and millions of dollars simply by effectively using Google, Youtube.com, Facebook and Instagram **ads.**

All you have to do to become proficient within these marketing and advertisement tools is to begin the process of getting your own **Google Ads certification** and your **Facebook business certification** online. Before being able to capitalize more effectively from these social media campaign advertisement tools. You will be in a much better position when utilizing these tools once you get these certifications under your belt and therefore, understand better how to properly and more effectively place or use your advertisement budget via all these social media platforms that are so popular nowadays.

Another significant and very important trend that we have seen in the social media and digital advertisement world is the use of the **influencer** stories to market or advertise products and services to the world. Influencers are the type of people who could be seen as trendsetters or sources of admiration and credibility to a lot of people. People like Michael Jordan, Keanu Reeves, Lady Gaga, or even Pope Francis on Twitter. These are all **social media influencers** who have thousands or millions of followers, who can, and will, charge you or your company a good price, to promote or mention your products and services via their social media channels for advertisement purposes. Of course, the people that I just mentioned might be very difficult to reach, but other less impactful influencer individuals might.

In that sense, *social media influencers* are people who are rated by the number of followers that they have. To give you a good example, within the Instagram social media world, the famous soccer Player *Cristiano Ronaldo* is the person with the largest amount of followers in the world with 152 million followers on Instagram. I am sure that Nike loves to see his Instagram pictures, every time he is wearing his Nike soccer boots, or a Nike T-shirt, in his relaxing days. In a way, influencers on social media are becoming more and more popular for *advertisement purposes,* than ever before. So that is a major point of interest, you might want to exploit, when using your marketing and advertisement budget wisely, depending on your target market.

Another very important element of the social media digital marketing tool kit, from the business side, is the *bidding process* that happens when two competing companies are bidding for the same audience, on a social media platform, as they are offering targeted ads to the same audience, in the same location, at the same time. Let's say that two very famous R&B singers will be singing in the city of Los Angeles, in different locations, on Sunday, December 31, this current year. There are millions and millions of people who like both artists, but Facebook and Instagram ads, use a bidding process, so that whoever bids more from those singers marketing teams, will get to obtain the higher return of investment for the advertisement investment. In other words, there is *a bidding tool*, or you could call it a bidding war, that can help you optimize your social media advertisement ROI if you win it.

Another way to explain it would be with the following example. If there is a street corner that has in one side of the street, a Starbuck coffee shop, and on the other side, a Dunkin Donuts coffee shop, Facebook will ask these companies to start a bidding process competing for the local advertisement audience around that corner's target market, and the company that pays the bigger bid, will win, when it comes to delivering the advertisement message to those coffee shops audiences. So in a way, there is a **competing process**, in these kinds of Facebook and Google ads scenarios.

Therefore, whether if you are selling R&B concert tickets, or a Coffee shop promo online, you'll have to **bid bigger** on your Facebook and Instagram business account, to get the largest amount of your target market to see your ads on those social media channels. And since in the world of business, as I mentioned before, it is not good to compete, but it is a lot better **to dominate**, whoever dominates the **bidding process** in these types of scenarios will always win.

Another quick tip about social media would be the following. When creating and developing your ads, you should also always try to **test your social media ads,** before investing heavily into them. Because chances are, when you place two ads, one ad is going to do better than the other. By offering two advertisement options to your prospect audiences, and by effectively using the analytical tools that these social media platforms have, you can determine which ad is obtaining a better response from your two test ad sets. Once you find out, which ad works better, cancel the other test ad, and **double down** your investment in the ad that is working well and will give you a higher return on investment. There are plenty of more tactics, and secrets that you could learn from these social media advertisement strategies, but teaching them to you will probably require of a book onto itself, so this is as far as we take you within the social media digital advertisement world.

Word of Mouth

It is hard to describe which one from the next two options, is the best-kept secret within the marketing and advertisement world. Is it the word of mouth method, the best marketing tool that has ever existed, or is it the email marketing function that I explained to you a little earlier in this chapter? The truth is that *social proof* counts, and social proof only means, that when someone else recommends, or suggest or highlights, the good things about a product or service, to other people, the other people will believe them and use or adopt that product and service into their lives with more confidence, joy and respect, that if nobody had talked to them about the product in the first place.

So in a way, the *word of mouth* works just like social proof. When your best friend tells you that his or her Coffee Maker Brand X works well, you will look for that very same Coffee Maker Brand X in the supermarket. And when another friend visits your house, and you share with them a coffee you made in your Brand X coffee machine and they like it, chances are they are going to purchase the Brand X coffee machine for themselves. And the *snowball effect* will continue afterward.

In that sense, the word of mouth continues to be the most effective way, to market your products and services still today, because nothing gives more confidence to the consumers than the *recommendation* from a *good friend* to buy or use your products and services. People love any type of products and services that have been recommended by their close friends and family.

In a very unique way, **word of mouth** marketing techniques, work similarly to the **peer pressure** technique. If everyone in your neighborhood drives and Mercedes Benz car, and you drive a Nissan Sentra, chances are that you will feel the pressure to buy a Mercedes Benz.

Copywriting

Another, very important **money making skill**, within the marketing and advertisement world, is the ability to create effective copywriting. Copywriting can be subjective, objective, direct, indirect, persuasive and influential. These are all good desired outcomes of effective writing. There is an element of timing, colors, design, poetry, and rhythm, to the words that you write, so that people can be more influenced or triggered by your words and what they are asking them to do. Whether if you are telling your audience to buy a car, or you are telling the audience to buy a dress, *your copywriting* message should be persuasive and concise.

Copywriting simply means "the ability to sell through text." And since, a good copy is the most direct *"Call To Action"* tool that you could ever use; it is good to learn the skills of effective copywriting.

The medium where the copy message is delivered also matters. Whether if the message is displayed on a billboard, or whether if the message is spoken on the radio, it also matters. It is not the same when you deliver a message on a Twitter account for instance than when you deliver a message on the newspaper. So, how you craft your message should be different, depending on the formats and requirements where you are delivering the message. There is a method to the madness, in every aspect of the copywriting world.

"Of course, copywriters are some of the highest-paid writers in the world. To become a proficient and profitable copy expert, you'll need to invest time and energy in studying the craft". For those reasons, if you want to make additional income, by offering your copywriting skills, I would definitely recommend to pursue that goal. The truth is that I had the opportunity to work as a copywriter for a popular cellular telephone company a few years back when I wrote my first book, "The Value of Peace." That is how I made some of my money back then.

Then, I began to write and direct video commercials for different clients across the South Florida region. And lastly, I noticed that I had definitely some excellent copywriting skills when I began to write songs in Spanish for other interpreters and people began to dig them. Of course, I may not have placed too much elegance in the copywriting of this book, mainly because that was not the main concern when I decided to write this book. But, **trust me,** if you like the title of my book "You deserve to be a millionaire"; it only means that I am great copywriting. Because chances are, the title of my book is what caught your attention in the first place. Don' you think? After all, isn't the title the first thing that you read in a book?

In that sense, "Copywriting is the process of writing advertising promotional materials. Copywriters are responsible for the text on brochures, billboards, websites, emails, advertisements, catalogs, and more. This text is known as "copy." Copy is everywhere — it's part of a $2.3 trillion industry worldwide. Unlike news or editorial writing, copywriting is all about *getting the reader* to *take action*. That action might be to purchase, opt-in, or engage with a product, service, or company. That's why a copywriter is often referred to as *"a salesman in print."*

Marketing Consultation Skills

Talking about an excellent money making skills, how about the ability to *sell your knowledge*. Whether if you are an expert on the marketing industry like I am, or whether if you are an expert in the medical industry or business law, how about putting your own consulting business. People are desperate for expert knowledge out there. In whatever area you specialize in. Why not selling it to them at a price that you deserve?

Of course, even having a good consulting business will require from you a good marketing manager or strategy. The truth is that how *people perceive you* or *see value* in your service, knowledge and expert advice, it's essential before you launch any consultation business online. If you are an expert in any field or line business, that could use the expert consultation business model, you could hire my company *"Five Star Media Management"* to help you in this process. Visit our website, www.fivestarmediamanagement.com, send us a quick message, and we'll begin the process of getting you online consultation website, ready to go.

Webinars

Another advantageous way of making money online in the digital market is by offering *training,* mentoring and *teaching* others your expert knowledge and skills via the use of the Internet.

You could use your expert knowledge and expert skills to create *webinars,* or offering your own online training courses, and even creating your **own online accredited university**; if you have the capital to do so of course. These are all huge profitable business in today's day and age. People nowadays, rather taking their university courses online, instead of attending every day to a physical school. For those reasons, there are some people making millions of dollars, out of this online business university models, because this is a new business opportunity that exists in the knowledge sector of the World Wide Web. These are all, digital products that offer expert knowledge with a price to the consumers. There is a consumer for every product in the market place. You could also deliver your training products via online conferences, but also via your own website, with training material at hand.

The truth is that the other day, I saw the story of one person, making one million dollars, out of **one single webinar**. Also, if you need help in the process of creating your own courses, or training products, you could also again, hire my company "five Star Media Management," to help you achieve your online digital educational leadership and entrepreneurial goals. We can help you with that.

Before I finish this chapter, let me give you one last paragraph on some critical E-commerce digital marketing platforms. Companies like Amazon.com have already incorporated a lot of these digital advertisement and marketing techniques that I explained to you in this chapter, within their online, operational workflow. Amazon.com, for instance, is the most successful e-commerce company in the world that specializes in selling products and services online, but also, this is a company that specializes in creating business partnerships with people like you. In the Amazon platform, for instance, you can **create your own online store,** and use all of their technological, logistical and marketing channels, to open up a business and sell your products and services to the entire world.

Chapter 5

Multiply money by investing it in the Stock Market

Principle # 5
" Use the Stock Market to your advantage"

They say that you need money in order to make money, and that is completely accurate. That is the nature of investing; to use your money to make more money. Because if you invest in something, anything, whatever it is, you are supposed to expect a return of investment, more famously known as ROI, from all your investments.

That is the nature of the Stock Market, or the Foreign Exchange Market (FOREX) and Futures Markets, to use your money to make more money and obtain a return of investment.

For that reason, Chapter 5 focuses on the creation of wealth, and the wealth management process through the use of the Stock, Futures, Forex, and Crypto currency markets. Because, if you ever want to obtain financial freedom, you need to at least know the basics of how the stock market operates, and how you can make lots of money via the use of these amazing platforms and tools available to you. Remember, the more tools you have at your disposal to make and maintain your money growing, the better.

Now, don't let anybody fool you, the stock market is a good thing and it's an excellent tool to make lots of money. I don't care what other people may say, or what other people may have experienced with it because to be honest with you, I have made a lot of money using the stock market. In fact, I wish I had learned about it a lot earlier in life and begin my investment activity at an earlier age. I would be a lot more rich and wealthy, had I learned to use the Stock Market from a very early age, obtaining my financial freedom sooner rather than later. Knowledge is power, and the more you know about the stock market, the better off you will be down the road.

Invest in your own education

Now remember, one of the key elements of this chapter is the word "learn", because it is a lot better and exciting that you learn how the stock market operates, instead of hiring somebody else to do it. Trust me, I give you this advice because having other people managing your money could lead to fraud issues, mismanagements of funds, legal issues and losing your money overall. That is why I always recommend that you learn to manage your money; no matter how long it takes, simply and plainly because nobody will take care of your money, the way you would, and the stock market is a great tool to invest and manage money for the rest of your life.

Now, I know, that this idea of learning something new may seem very challenging at first, but don't hesitate. Once you make your first successful investment, you will feel a lot more confident and optimistic to keep learning and digging more into the deep world of possibilities that this tool gives you.

As mentioned before, knowledge is power. That is absolutely true in this case. Of course, there are certain types or kinds of *knowledge* that are more powerful than others, or useful and practical than others, especially, when it comes to making money and trying to become a *millionaire*. Because, even though knowledge about history or science, or geography is likely to add a lot of strategic perspective to your mind, knowledge about finance, accounting, and the market behavior might improve your chances to accumulate more wealth than others over a large period of time. Not only because, these set of finance and wealth management skills have a larger pool of *high paying* jobs, but also, because you'll have a more specialized skill set to manage your money and multiply it over time.

Keep Control of your Money

One of the best wealth creation and investment portfolio management tips that I can give you is to keep control of your investments. Because the reality is that if you transfer, some of that control to other individuals, they will most likely, only be looking for their best interest when it comes to managing your money. That is a realist perspective of looking at life. "Everybody is looking only for their best interest". Of course, delegation of authority is very important for a Millionaire who has a lot of capital and multiple businesses, but there are some executive decision that you better be in *control* of. For those reasons, one of the key elements of a successful investment portfolio manager includes having the ability to control your investments. Therefore, we advise you, to invest preferably in your most useful and fruitful investment vehicles that you already know and have given you a very profitable ROI, or high return of investment. But also, if you are a new investor, do not trust, third-party financial managers or executives with your money, who won't be looking for your benefit in the first place. So unless you believe that you have come to a win-win agreement with them, where if you win, they win type of agreement, go ahead and invest with them, but even then, I would not trust anybody with my money, to manage it, or invest it for me, without me having the *last word* on how the money is invested.

Let me be clear, I am not saying that you cannot or should not use or replicate the activity of some of the most talented investors and wealth managers in today day and age. On the contrary, if you are investing your money in an Exchange Traded Fund (ETF) managed by some of the most successful wealth managers of the twentieth first century, such as Catherine Woods and her ETF's from Ark Invest; you are likely to be very successful. But even in this case, you would be in charge of your money by investing it in those ETF's, because you can buy or sell, the shares in those ETF's, at any point in time during the market hours. So, it is always better that you be in control. By the way, I highly recommend that you follow Catherine Woods, from Ark Invest and what companies her firm is invested in. She has been one of the most successful investors and wealth managers from recent years.

What is an ETF?

An ETF, or Exchange Traded Fund, "is a type of security that involves a collection of securities—such as stocks—that often tracks an underlying index, although they can invest in any number of industry sectors or use various strategies. ETFs are traded throughout the day just like ordinary stocka"[14].

In more simple words, an ETF is an investment fund composed of multiple stocks managed by a specific agency, or company, that can be used to track any specific industry, or can be used as a benchmark of the overall stock market. A good example of an industry related ETF's could be the one recently launched by Catherine Woods (ARKX), built to invest in the space exploration related companies. On the other hand, some of the most common ETF's used to track the overall performance of the stock market are the S&P 500, the Nasdaq, and the Dow Jones.

Tactics & Strategies in the Stock Market

The fact is that there are multiple tactics and strategies to make money in the stock market. And you can apply them in different shapes and forms according to your knowledge base and your level of risk tolerance. But also depending on whether if you are a long-term investor or a short- term investor. Short-term investors are also known as day or swing traders.

If you are a long-term investor, for example, one of the most common ways to invest your money is to buy a stock at a low price at an early date and then sell it at a much higher price once the stock has mature on a later date. Using the principle number one of this book, which is the principle of arbitrage, which means to buy low and sell high, you can buy a stock at a low price and then sell it at a higher price in the future. After all, the long-term trend of the market does goes up and higher over the long term. That is, of course, if you choose a good stock, or if you buy a benchmark ETF's such as the S&P 500, the NASDAQ, the DOW JONES or the RUSSELL 2000. If you buy one share in those ETFs, over the long term, you will always win. Or if you buy a good stock, for instance, let us pretend that you bought 1000 shares of Amazon, when the stock was at $15.00 USD at an initial investment of $15000.00 dollars. That initial investment would have transformed you into a millionaire in today's day and age given that the price of an Amazon stock today, Jan 18, 2021 is $3100.00. Your initial investment of $15000.00 would have transformed into $3,100,000.00 over the period of twenty years making you a millionaire over the long term. So that is a long-term strategic view.

Now, the fact is that the market does goes up over the long-term. However, there are some periods in time, when the market goes down. These are also known as Market corrections. Long term investors don't tend to look at these down times, as a major challenge to their portfolios, even when there are strong market corrections, or market crashes, because their investment strategy has a long term view, and remember, the trend does goes up over the long term.

Note: Long-term investors do not ever sell their stocks during a market correction. Panic selling is usually made by new; non-experienced investors. The fact is that some of the more savvy investors buy more stocks during the market corrections because the stocks are cheaper during these periods of time.

What is a Stock?

A Stock is defined as "an equity investment [or share] that represents part *ownership* in a corporation and entitles you to part of that corporation's earnings and assets. *A common stock* gives shareholders voting rights but no guarantee of dividend payments. *Preferred stock* provides no voting rights but usually guarantees a dividend payment"[15]. Now, it is important to remember that not all stocks give dividends. "The term *dividend* may be defined as the return that a shareholder gets from the company, out of its profits, on his shareholdings." [16].

It is important to keep in mind the following. You can make money out of every stock in the market. No matter whether if you have preferred or common stocks, as long as you buy them at a low price, and then sell them at a higher price over time. That is the nature of the long-term strategy. Dividend stocks, will also give you that additional incentive to own them, because they give you an additional gain over the profits of the company, however, those dividend values are different from company to company.

The Market goes Up & Down & You Can Make Money in Both Ways

In the stock market, you can make money when the market goes up, or when the market goes down. Like I said, it all depends on the level of knowledge that you have and your risk tolerance, but also on the type of strategy you have.

Making money when the market goes down is usually achievable via the means of some short-term Bearish strategies. Bearish means the trend and sentiment of the market is going down. Bullish, means the trend and sentiment of the stock market is going up.

In a given scenario that you know a company stock, or if you happen to know that the stock market in general is going down (Bearish), or that there is a market correction happening in the near future, you can do two things in order to make money, but these are both short term and risky strategies.

You can engage in a "Short Selling Strategy", where you (1) borrow the stock you want to bet against, from your brokerage account, 2) Immediately sell the shares you have borrowed, (3) wait for the stocks to fall and then buy the shares back at a new lower price (4) you return the shares to the brokerage account you borrowed from and win & pocket the difference.

However, this short selling strategy can only be applied by using a margin account, which is an account your brokerage firm grants you to lend you money for investment purposes. To be more precise, "a margin account is a brokerage account in which the broker lends the customer cash to purchase stocks or other financial products. The loan in the account is collateralized by the securities purchased and cash you have in your account, and comes with a periodic interest rate" [17]. I don not recommend people to use margin accounts in their investment strategies.

The second form to make money when a stock goes down in price, is via the use of an option "Put" strategy, where you can bet, that a stock will go down in price in a given specific point in time, based on your judgment. If your judgement is correct, you will make money as the price of the share goes down and reach your called predicted "Put price".

Options Trading

"Options" are advanced trading tools that allow the investor to make a lot more money with a lower cost of investment. However, they are riskier in the sense that you need to have a lot more skills and knowledge as a day trader, than as a long-term investor. But they are also riskier because you can loose all your initial investment. The fact is that there is statistical data that shows that, "90% of Day Traders tend to loose money over the long term". This could be related to the higher number of daily transactions and the increase amount of risk tolerance over time.

The fact is that in order to make successful gains using option trades you must accurately predict how the price of a specific stock is going to behave within the future, or a certain period of time. In this case, time is very important, or sensitive because the value of the option decreases over time. For example, if on any given Monday, you think that the price of stock (A), currently priced at $1.00 is going to go up to $1.25 by the end of the week, you can buy an option "call", saying that the stock is going to hit a price of $1.25 by Friday. If the price of stock (A) reaches $1.25 on Monday, you will make a lot more money, but if it reached the price of $1.25 on Tuesday, of Wednesday, or Thursday, or Friday, you will make a lot less money, as time moves forward, because the value of any option trade, whether if it is a put, or a call, decreases over time. Just be aware of this fact.

Note: Most options trades have expiration days on Fridays. For example: If you place an option trade for the length of a month from today, that option will expire the Friday, 4 weeks from now. So time, also plays a significant role in options trading. That is why this type of trading has a lot more risk, than a regular long-term investment, because time also plays a significant role in it. Therefore, the faster that the stock reaches your price target the more money you will make. The later that your stock reaching you price target, the less money that you will make. And if the stock never reaches your price prediction, you will lose all your money.

Options Technicalities

Technically speaking, "Options are *contracts* that give the owner the right to buy or sell an asset at a fixed price for a specific period of time. That period could be as short as a day or as long as a couple of years, depending on the type of options contract. As mentioned before, as time moves forward, the value of the option decreases, since time does also plays a significant role in options trading.

There are only two types of standard option contracts: *calls and puts*. A *call option* contract gives the owner the right to purchase 100 shares of a specific security at a specific price within a specific time frame. But also a call option means you predict that the price of the stock will go up to the specific price you think it will go up to.

On the opposite side, a *put option* contract gives the owner the right to sell 100 shares of a specified security at a specified price within a specified time frame, but also, a put option means that you are betting that the price of the stock will go down to an specific price within a specific moment in time.

So it is true, in the stock market, you can make money from its volatility, when the market goes down, or when the market goes up, or when the shares of a company you own, goes up or when they go down. Like I said, it all depends on the level of knowledge that you have and your risk tolerance.

These are advanced trading techniques that are usually used by very experienced, savvy traders, known as day or swing traders and both strategies involve a higher level of risk tolerance and deep knowledge about the stock behavior, business intelligence analysis and other very important variables impacting the stock price.

Options trading, can give you a very high reward on one hand, but on the other hand, you can loose all you investment a lot faster. Of course, good timing is extremely important in these types of trading, as well as the sense of urgency any individual or person may have when it comes to becoming wealthy. Let us not forget, that there is a direct relationship between timing, urgency, and risk when it comes to investing your money. The faster that you may want your return of investment, the quicker might be to lose your initial investment. In other words, the shorter the time, you want to obtain your gains, the higher the risk of losing your investment. Or simply saying it, short time investments might give you a higher return on investment, but they also will give you the highest exposure to risk in the market place.

Investment Decisions

There is a lot of data available in the world out there to make good, better-informed, well educated and reliable, *investment decisions* in the market place. This data is based not only on qualitative and quantitative intelligence that other experts may have placed out there in the market but also variables such as consumer demand, market speculation, product or service type, supply, production capacity, earnings reports, government regulations, and other political and security variables affecting the company or the stock where you want to invest. All of these market behavior patterns and business intelligence information are all traceable nowadays, by the very unique brokerage accounts or firms that offer you electronic trading capacity in today's day and age.

In fact, brokerage accounts and specialized internet trading platforms such as TD Ameritrade, Robinhood, Webull, Interactive Traders, E-trade and Robinhood, come with several market intelligence analytical tools and market alerts that are useful for every trader, from every experience level. The truth is that in today's technological world, we can trade commission free, from our own mobile phones, using the mobile apps that these brokerage accounts offer, for free. But they also offer us the latest news about the market, the companies and trends in the market place. The Internet has opened the capabilities to traders to perform faster and better company research and market research in ways that it was impossible in the past.

"Risk comes from not knowing what you are doing" according to *Warren Buffett*. Therefore, finding out what tools can help you understand all these variables better so that you can *reduce risk*, is a critical activity for you to make, to better improve your chances of making the right investments and profitable decisions at the right point in time. Knowledge is what can and will give you the *clarity*, certainty and competitive advantage and a clear pathway to success. Without investment knowledge, or market analytics and intelligence, all you will be doing when or during your investing process is gambling.

Timing is also a very important element of success when it comes to investing. Just as important as knowledge, because timing is what determines when and how you make the decision, *to execute*, either to *buy* a stock or *sell* a stock at the right point in time. Timing is the activity of making an *executive decision*, to determine, when to buy and when to sell, or when to invest and when to stop your investment.

Think about the 2008 real estate market crash for example. There was a *bubble* in the American market that was built upon granting undeserved credit, to millions and millions of people to buy their houses, in an inflated seller market. Houses prices were as high as they have never been, and people with bad credit and two jobs, where applying to buy half of million dollar houses, and they were obtaining the loans and the credit. Therefore, when all these buyers were not able to pay for their mortgages, the economy collapsed, and the market and people within the United States went nuts. There were people committing suicide because they had lost all their economic or financial assets in this market crash. Crazy right?

However, there were only a few *smart* individuals, who made billions or millions of dollars from this collapse, in a time were most of the American people and American investors, lost money. These brilliant investors who were able to make a lot of money, and I mean a lot of money, had some very unique *skill sets* that the majority of the people within the United States did not have.

First of all, they applied the principle number one of this book, which is to *buy low and sell high*. Always remember the principle number one of this book. But also, just like Warrant Buffett says "be fearful when others are greedy, and be greedy when others are fearful." *Warren Buffett*. He further down explains, that when his janitor is buying any specific shares, he sells those shares from his portfolio. Because, that only means, that there is a market correction that is about to take effect or speculation is so high, that it has reached to the masses and everybody is buying at this point in time the shares, even his janitor. When a phenomenon like that happens, it only means that the market is about to correct itself.

In that sense, a lot of smart investors win a lot of capital, buy and invest their money, during the *market correction* phase, meaning, when the market crashed, and all shares went down to their lowest possible prices. Because the principle number one of this book will always work which is to *buy low and sell high*. Because a market share that you buy in its lowest price can only go up, there are always a lot of opportunities to make a lot of money when the market corrects itself. Meaning, buying in *the bear market*, because when *the bull market* is up, there is a very low margin for substantial gains, but also, the shares are as expensive as they will ever be, nearly at their price peak point.

People like Warren Buffett and John Paulson who bet against the U.S housing Market in 2008 and made $2.5 US Billion dollars during the *same crisis*, or people like Jamie Dimon, who as the CEO of JP Morgan "bought to acquire Bear Stearns and Washington Mutual, which were two financial institutions brought to ruins by huge bets on U.S. housing"[9]. They were able to capitalize in the U.S 2008 financial crisis in ways that nobody else imagined. *Mergers and acquisitions*, which can be excellent tools, for high return investment channels, were very profitable for Jamie Dimon in this case, because "JPMorgan acquired Bear Stearns for $10 a share, or roughly 15% of its value from early March 2008. In September of that year, it also acquired Washington Mutual"[10] and JP Morgan, was able to triple its *equity value* and made the CEO of this company a very wealthy man in the process. So in a way, there is always a profit to be made out of a crisis, and I do not mean it in a bad way. Don't go out to the streets inventing a crisis, but make sure that you position your self wisely when it comes to investment during a crisis. You can win from it, or you can lose from it. The key, I would say, is to do the exact opposite of what the majority of the people in the market place are doing. If the majority of the people are selling, you buy, and if the majority of the people are buying, you sell.

Like I say, the principle number one of this book will always apply. *Buy low, sell high.* And unfortunately, this principle goes sometimes goes hand to hand with a crisis. People sell low during a crisis because there is a financial emergency that they want to solve. Kind of like the principle of buying houses from distressed individuals, if you have the shark tank mentality. And I mean it, in a very respectful way from only a pragmatic, realistic perspective. The reality is that the principle number one of this book is very intertwined with principle number five of this book, which is to use the stock market to make money. *Buy low and sell high, at the right moment in time.* Especially if you are investing in a highly volatile market, such as Forex, the Stock Market, and other short-term investment avenues, but also in any long-term investment option. Always apply these two principles in tandem.

Also, the truth is that there is a lot of economic value to time. Every second counts and the market place accounts for it. That is why, variables such as *inflation*, carry a very significant cost, but also opportunities in the market place. That is also, why, people and banks make a lot of *"interest"* profit from lending money. Take the *"compound interest"* for example. This is an interest accrual vehicle that multiplies your possible return of investment over time, in incredible ways. That is, when you are the loan provider, of course. If you are the loan receiver, on the other hand, it will multiply your loan cost over time. The truth is that compound interest is a loan interest multiplier in both ways, for a loan provider, or the loan receiver. You will make a lot of money if you are the loan provider over time, and you will lose a lot of money if you are the loan receiver over time.

The bottom line is that *time has a lot of value*, and so does timing. The timing of your investment is what is going to determine whether if you are going to make a successful investment decision or not. And, as in many other industries, people will usually make the profit at the point of purchase of the asset or time of effect of their investment, because when they buy their investment opportunities at a low price and wait until the price of the product or commodity goes up to sell, then, that is when they make their money. When you buy your items at a low price at the time of the purchase and sell them for a profit, at a later date. This is also known as a "*Capital Gains.*" If you are a *Capital Gains* type of investor, you are making money on the upside of a product, by buying low and selling it, at a higher price in the market place.

Take a house, or a real estate investment asset for example. Let's say that you bought a property at the beginning of the year 2000 for USD 70,000.00 USD in the Wynwood district in the city of Miami. Today, in 2021, that same house, or piece of land, will cost more than a Million dollars to whoever wants to purchase it, just because you bought that property in a district that exploded in value a few years later but also, because time and inflation augmented the value of your house or property over time. Time will always add value to your property, because inflation is a phenomenon that appears to be continuous, but also because a property usually gains value over time.

Market Speculation

Speculation is also a beautiful factor, that plays a very important or significant role during the investment process, but speculation can only be fought against, but having the proper knowledge and market insightful intelligence data that can remove speculation and increase your sense of *certainty* in whatever type of investment you are trying to make.

Take the Bitcoin phenomena for example. Early in 2013, I went to an early year investment *conference* during the first week of the year in the city of Fort Lauderdale, Florida, to get some insightful information on the new years investment trends. Of course, the first thing that they suggested to us was to invest in Bitcoin, Blockchain technologies and even though you might consider this as a Joke, they advise us to invest in Marihuana stocks. Go ahead; laugh it up. At that point in time, the *Bitcoin* was selling at *$13.62 USD*.

Little did I know, that by May 2013, four months later; the price of Bitcoin was going to be sold at $133.03 USD. A *10 X* value increase in the short period of four to five months. Of course, everybody went crazy, by the date of November 29, 2013, a few months later, when that same Bitcoin that used to cost $13.62 USD at the beginning of the year, was now at a price of *$1,242.00 USD*. Nearly a *100 X* value *gain* for a lot of people who had invested heavily in Bitcoin, like my good friend Mike Smith. The truth is that this good friend of mine who had bought 1000 Bitcoins at price of $13.62 USD, was now a Millionaire, by Nov 2013 (*eleven months later*) with a profit of $1,228,380.00 USD, just by investing $13,620.00 dollars in Bitcoin based on that *one educated advice* that we received at that one Fort Lauderdale *conference*.

Of course, that was not the end of that Bitcoin story. As we mentioned before in one of the previous chapters of this book, *a good story will always sell,* and the Bitcoin story had just become a fantastic story for a lot of people. So much so, that the *Bitcoin* story became one of the leading speculative stories of all times, via all the newspapers and all the major financial newsrooms.

And you know what speculations can do right? Well, it adds *gas to a fire*. That is the purpose of speculation, to give value and a trending topic, to something that may, or may not, increase or add value over the future. In can also be exemplified by a gossiping story that everybody hears about and nobody knows if what has been talked about is based on any tangible or absolute certainty. Speculation is just that, a *trending topic* without absolute *certainty*.

The problem is that people who have no idea about that specific topic being speculated or talked about see the information that is being speculated about as tangible information, and they are willing to make an investment decision based on those speculative stories.

Take the story of Juan Diaz for example, a Hospitality Major student, who placed all his saving into the Bitcoin platform, when the price the Bitcoin was at $1,099.00 USD at the beginning dates of January 2014. He was expecting based on the *speculation rhetoric* he had heard about Bitcoin in the news, but also at some of the most influential financial newspapers in the U.S that the price of Bitcoin was going to increase during that same year by another 10 X margin. But the truth is that unfortunately, all the opposite happened. By the end of 2015, the price of Bitcoin had decreased to $383.00 USD, and he had to sell his Bitcoins, based an unforeseen emergency that he had not accounted for. Therefore, he lost most of his money in the process. This is truly a sad story. He ended up losing a good portion of his investment.

My friend Mike Smith on the other hand, based on the informed, *analytical information* or *intelligence* he had received, but also, based on his diversification investment strategy he had utilized, was able to continue to keep his Bitcoin portfolio for a long time, until the end of the year 2018, when he sold his *1000 Bitcoins*, for the price of $18,420.00 USD *each* — making a substantial millionaire profit of

$18,406,380.00. USD. All these profit margins from that initial $13,620.00 dollars investment. What a great story. All because he had applied his *timing right*, based on a well-supported insightful data analysis that some of his advisers were giving to him. In a way, Mike's story is a very unique story, of how luck, useful information, and making the right decision at the *right point in time*, can make you or keep you a millionaire. I guess a lot of us will have to wait until another major investment opportunity like this one occurs. I am sure, another Initial Coin Offering (ICO) is not going to cut the Bitcoin experience, but there are certainly a lot of *IPO's* out there, that could make the cut, depending on what piece of solution or technologies these companies are providing in the market place.

The truth is that speculation will always have a *key role* in the stock or investment market, but the truth is that it is always better to lower your risk in any type of investment by conducting your *homework*, and making sure that you have the long and short term strategic commitment to stick to your guns and your investment until *the time is right to sell*. A good piece of advice is to *diversify* your portfolio even in the type of industry you are investing in because it is always better to be prepared than sorry. Remember, it is always good to diversify your entire portfolio if you can. And one more thing, always, trust you educated gut, if you can.

Initial Public Offerings (IPO's)

Initial Public Offerings are an excellent mechanism to invest in a new company and gain some profit over the short and long term. Of course, you will have to conduct your *homework*, before investing in an IPO to make sure you are making the right kind of investment. Some initial public offerings (IPOs), such as the *Apple IPO* of December 12, 1980, made instant *millionaires*. Apple for example, "launched the IPO (initial public offering) of its stock, selling 4.6 million shares at $22 per share with the stock symbol "AAPL" on the NASDAQ market. The shares sold out almost immediately, and the IPO generated more capital than any IPO since Ford Motor Company in 1956. Instantly, about *300 millionaires were created*, some 40 of which were Apple employees and investors. That is more millionaires than any company in history had produced at that time. Steve Jobs, the largest shareholder, made $217 million dollars alone. By the end of the day, the stock had increased in value by almost 32% to close at $29, leaving the company with a market value of $1.778 billion"[18].

Of course, this Apple IPO experience is not always replicated by other companies. The fact is, that this is an exception to the rule. Initial public offerings can be *risky* because, despite the efforts made by the company to disclose information to the public in order to obtain the green light on the IPO by the SEC, there is still a high degree of *uncertainty* as to whether a company's management will perform the necessary duties to propel the company forward. So, therefore, make sure, that you get you quantitative and qualitative homework done before investing in any IPO. Make sure that the IPO you invest in has a bright future.

Currency Trading / Forex Trading

Currency, or Forex trading, as it is called, is not for beginners. However, "the currency market, or Forex (FX), is the *largest* investment market in the world and continues to grow annually. On April 2010, the Forex market reached $4 trillion in daily average turnover, an increase of 20 percent since 2007"[19].

There are multiple different variables that may affect the value of any specific currency. Among them, the local interest rates of the currency and the political environment in any country can suddenly change or modify a country's currency value. We definitely recommend that you invest in this kind of trading, only if you know how to play the Forex game.

Gold

"Gold can be purchased directly or indirectly. You can put a box of the metal under your bed if a direct purchase suits your fancy, or you can invest in the stock of a company involved in the gold mining business. You can also opt to invest in a mutual fund or exchange-traded fund that specializes in gold. There, you have the option of an actively managed fund that offers the service of a professional money manager or a passive, index-based product.

Gold is also a popular inflation hedge. Investors tend to turn to this precious metal during inflationary times, causing its price to rise. While silver and other metals also tend to gain value during inflationary times, gold is generally the headline-grabbing investment, with the price of gold shooting up when inflation is notably present.

Like real estate and gold, the price of oil moves with inflation. This cost increase flows through to the price of gasoline and then to the price of every consumer good transported by truck or produced by a machine that is powered by gas (crop pickers, tractors, etc.). Since modern society cannot function without fuel to move vehicles filled with consumers and consumer goods, oil has a strong appeal to investors when inflation is rising. Other commodities such as cotton, orange juice, and soybeans also tend to increase in price when inflation rises". [20]

Foreign Emerging Markets

A country experiencing a growing economy can be an ideal investment opportunity for you if or when the conditions are right. As an investor, you can always buy government bonds, stocks or sectors with that country experiencing hyper-growth or exchange-traded funds that represent a growing sector of stocks. Again, the political environment of the country where you decide to invest can suddenly change or modify your investment's value. Therefore, there is a level of risk in these types of investments, depending on the political and economic condition of the country where you are investing. Always remember in that sense, that investing is also a matter of trust. Always think, whether if you trust the investment vehicle, the intelligence data, or any other type of insightful information that is given to you, or not, in order to make that investment decision. If you trust the source, the chances are that you will be making a good investment.

Inflation-Indexed Bonds

"Inflation often causes interest rates to rise. Because interest rates and bond prices have an inverse relationship, inflation makes existing bond holdings worth less to investors. To overcome this obstacle, investors can purchase bonds that are inflation-indexed.

In the United States, Treasury Inflation Protected Securities are a popular inflation-indexed investment. *TIPS*, as they are commonly called, are pegged to the Consumer Price Index. When the Index rises, so does the value of an investment in TIPS. Not only does the base value increase but, since the interest paid is based on the base value, the amount of the interest payment rises with the base value increase. Other varieties of inflation-indexed bonds are also available, including those issued by other countries"[21].

Cash Flow Investing

You can think of *cash flow* investing the same way you think about dividends with stocks. At some interval, whether it is monthly, quarterly, semi-annually or annually, you *will receive* regular cash distributions from your investment.

You are *buying* a portion, or all, of an asset that can be *leased* or otherwise used to *generate* income. With real estate investing, cash flow is the result of proceeds from *rent payments*. Let's take a multi-family apartment building as an example. Say the property has 60 units and each unit rents for $1,000 per month. If we assume an expense ratio of 40%, the net income per month on that property is $36,000. While it is always a good idea to keep some portion of that net income in reserves, the remainder of the income is available for distribution, in this example, $36,000.

"Real estate is just one type of cash flow investment. Other examples include investing in *ATM machines or Laundromats* - purchasing any asset that provides regular cash income"[22].

To conclude this chapter, always remember the following. Wealth is not created. *Wealth is transferred*. There is a lot of wealth in the world; all you have to do is being prepared and open to receive it. Last tip, Keep 10 % of your wealth, in cash, liquidity. You never know, when you might need that cash.

Venture Capital Investing

Investing in new startups can be risky. Mainly because a lot of these startups are innovative companies that are particularly unstable and they carry up a lot of uncertainty around them. The truth is that many *startups* fail, but a few of them are able to offer high-demand products and services that the public wants and needs. Even if a startup's product is desirable, poor management, poor marketing efforts, and even a bad location can deter the success of a new company.

Therefore, you will also have to conduct your homework before becoming an *Angel Investor* or venture capitalist. The risk is pretty high, but the rewards can also be *extraordinary*. Many startups are built by great people; with extraordinary ideas, but it often turns out that these people are not business-minded at all. Therefore, you will need to conduct additional research to ensure the viability of a brand new company. Venture capital investments usually have very high minimums, which can be *challenging* for some investors. If you are considering putting your money into a venture capital fund or investment, make sure to do your due *diligence.*

Business Acquisitions as High Return Investments

There are multiple other high return investment strategies available out there, depending on what type of investor you are. Of course, you have to always consider what are your strengths, weaknesses, opportunities, and threats, when it comes to investment. Kind of like a *SWOT* analysis report, in terms of your portfolio management history. What type of investment vehicles do you thrive on, or what kind of investment platform is your forte, and how could you maximize those strengths and investment opportunities and returns based on your own self-assessment test.

Some very successful investors like Warren Buffett for instance, are good at buying *Businesses* that are not adequately managed. They buy these businesses for a very low price, and then they go ahead to fix those businesses, change their business model, hire a new management team, and transform their newly purchased business into an extremely profitable business. This type of strategy in the Business Management world is called a *Business Acquisition* practice. For example, If you have a big construction company that is doing fairly well, with multiple assigned projects for the long future, and all of the sudden, you discover that one of your vendors or suppliers who sells you the cement for your construction projects, is selling their business due to a mismanagement process, buying that cement provider company, could be a good business acquisition investment opportunity for you to follow, if you have multiple projects to come, and you want to supply all your projects with your own cement company at a lower price. Of course, the decision to *buy or acquire* a new business is not that easy to make. You have to make sure that the *numbers are right*, and conduct a breakeven analysis, an Internal Rate of Return study, a future profit projection of the company, plus a company assets analysis, and many more studies and professional reviews in order to make sure that this is a profitable move. If it is not a profitable move, then, all you will be doing is losing money and gaining a new headache.

But the truth is that there are also a lot of distressed sellers in the business world who want to sell their businesses right now, but also, there are a lot of business owners who just want to retire, travel and visit their grandchildren.

Therefore, if you consider that you have the skills, knowledge, and capital to make of that business purchase a profitable investment, buying a company, that has some tangible and profitable financial assets could be a good move, if you are *confident* that you can maximize the gains of this transaction and obtain a high return investment out of this purchase.

Let's look back into the *Jamie Dimon* example, the current CEO of JP Morgan, for instance, where "JPMorgan acquired Bear Stearns for $10 a share, or roughly 15% of its value from early March 2008. In September of that year, it also acquired Washington Mutual banks"[12]. Because of those very precise *acquisition executive decisions*, JP Morgan was able to triple its *equity value* and make the CEO of the company very wealthy in the process as well. Bearn Stearns and Washington Mutual had to sell their companies, due to a distressed *crisis situation* that ended up being very profitable for JP Morgan. Of course, this is not the case for every business acquisition transaction that has happened in the market place, some of them, if not conducted properly, can end up bringing a substantial loss for the investor, so you as the investor will have to make your *homework*. The truth is that there are a lot of companies in the market place, just in that same situation of needing to sell. Therefore, if you see a business opportunity that fits you well and you have the capital, by all means, go ahead, make the purchase and implement your successful business models that you believe will make that company profitable, or assign the right *team of managers* who will take that company to afloat.

Other types of Investments

The truth is that if you really want to make a lot of money, you will have to find a mechanism that will make you money while you *sleep*. That is the bottom line. There are many investment vehicles and products and services out there that can do this for you. Of course, they are difficult to follow or catch, because otherwise, everybody will be conducting those types of investments.

Book and Music *Royalties*, for example, used to be one of those sleep Money making mechanisms that existed in the market place. However, music royalties seem to be a thing of the past, as a money creation *tool* that would make artist money while they slept in today's day and age, because the digital world has music artists, nowadays, making money out of their live performances at small venues and large scale *concerts* instead of out of their royalties revenue from online streams. Of course, there are still a lot mechanisms to make money out of your digital music by selling it online, and getting streaming and *advertisement revenue*, but the profit margins are not as substantial as they used to be in the past, when people had to buy a whole album, instead of getting their songs online for free at places like youtube.com, or Spotify. *Book sales* have also declined, substantially, since the *peer-to-peer* computer networking trends and phenomenon, showed up, and people began to share books online instead of buying them. Of course, Amazon.com took advantage of that change within the computer technology trends and invested all its time and efforts, into the e-commerce platforms. That is how Amazon.com began to make a substantial profit; by selling *books and e-books* online.

Nobody would have thought back when Amazon.com first started, that this company would become the most profitable company in the year 2018. So the truth is that there is still a lot of money to be made out of book sales, but it all depends on how you market your books, and your digital and non-digital marketing strategy. The truth is that if you want to get the largest amount of people to buy your products online in today's day an age, you will have to implement a good *marketing* strategy. For those reasons, you have to read, chapter four of this book, which talks about *marketing like a millionaire*. Book products will always give you *credibility* so always think about that additional value when thinking about investing your time in writing a book. People will begin to see you as an expert, which can add value to your time for expert consultation purposes. You can develop an expert consulting firm, just to add an additional stream of income to your persona. Furthermore, if your book becomes a best seller, *one simple* book could make you a millionaire. The same goes for the music artists, *one single song* could make you a millionaire, but for those purposes, you would have to be a really good artist and have a great marketing manager in order to achieve those goals.

Also, the creation of *digital products* and *digital storefronts* is a great strategy to sell products and services online while you are sleeping. Digital products are usually cheaper and easier to make, so you will be saving a lot of money in manufacturing cost. But just keep in mind; there is a direct relationship between your marketing efforts and the sales of your products and services in the digital and non-digital fronts. You will need to have effective and persuasive selling techniques but also extremely good action calling *landing pages* in your websites, in order to sell your products and services online in the best and most effective, possible way. You can buy some of my other books, products, songs and services at www.fabianavilastore.com, for example.

Chapter 6

Embrace the Uncomfortable

Success Exists Outside Your Comfort Zone

Yes, you have heard it before. Success happens only outside of your comfort zone and that it's simply, **completely true**. No one, who has made into the history books in the world, across time, has done it while sleeping in the couch. No one. All of the men and women out there, who have reached, feel and touch the stars and have obtained the pleasures and the fruits of success, mostly have obtained it because they live or have lived *outside* of their comfort zone for a great portion of their lives. That is the greatest common denominator among all of them. That is their common *unifier*. All of those successful people out there who have accomplished something worth of embracement, honor, and respect, one day decided, that they were no longer going to be mediocre, fearful, and comfortable just like the common people, but on the other hand, they decided that they were going to be exceptional and unique leaders on their own unique fields, while living outside of their comfort zone every day, until one day the uncomfortable, became their **comfort zone**. Until one day, unconsciously, *success* became their comfort zone, and they reached or accomplished their *dreams and goals*.

People like Tony Robbins, Steve Jobs, Barack Obama, people like Nelson Mandela, to include Donald Trump, have obtained what they dreamed because they went full throttle at it, they **burned the boat**, as they say. They gave themselves, not alternative roadmaps, but they got themselves, a one-way ticket to success, no matter what. They were **certain** about their motives, **certain** about their north. And in the face of uncertainty, they **conquered their fears** and reached to the *"Mountain Top."* They in effect, impacted or changed the world, in ways no other group of people has.

In that respect, there is no doubt, that achieving your dreams and goals is what you want to do, but make **no mistake**, achieving them can be **uncomfortable**. However, when the uncomfortable becomes your comfort zone; that is when you have really **achieved success**. When public speaking becomes second nature, when **leading** a group of leaders is your day to day activity, when you are managing director of a hedge fund, or becoming the greatest social media influencer of all times, or the greatest songwriter, or the CEO of a disruptive company like Elon Musk, or even the President of the free world, just like any of the presidents of the United States of America, who have to make the **toughest** decisions in the world. All of them have passed and fight through their **discomfort zone**, to become numb to critics, and understand, that not everyone is going to like you, not everyone is going to support you. Not everything is going to be easy. Not everyone is going to please you, and not everyone is going to answer the phone. The truth is that you will **never be liked** or accepted by everyone in the world, some people will love you, and some people will hate you. That is the bottom line.

Of course, there is an element of discipline, hard work, talent, cleverness, guts, boldness, consistency, follow up, and sometimes luck, to achieve great things and moreover success in life, but all of them, require a level of *discomfort* at some point in time in order for you to take your game into *the next level*. At some point in time, when reaching for the stars, you will begin to be challenged, by the nature of the game, by the haters, by life, by society, by your boss, maybe by your coworkers, and your friends, and even by your own *self-doubts and fears*, because at the end we are our own biggest enemies. And you will have to learn how to manage those discomfort situations.

Of course, this advice of living outside of your comfort zone does not apply to any of your investment practices or portfolio management processes. On the contrary, *when investing*, you should always invest in things or investment vehicles that you are comfortable with, because, the truth is that *comfort* comes from knowledge, certainty, and confidence. And *confidence* will make you comfortable. In a good way, this is a *reciprocal* relationship. Having insightful and expert knowledge and advice, but also investment *experience*, should and will always give you confidence, and confidence will make you *comfortable*. That would be the ideal scenario. Of course, always keeping in mind the principle of portfolio diversification when investing. Meaning, you can leave a very small portion of your investment capital, for riskier investment opportunities, but just a *small* portion of it. The truth is that I know a lot of wealthy people, whose main purpose in life is only to *maintain* their wealth, so they focus more on long-term investments that are *safe and effective* over the long term, such as real estate, instead of gambling.

But outside of the portfolio investment wealth creation process, there are several *elements* within the business world, that requires for you to live outside of your comfort zone, such as *public speaking*, leading a group of leaders, negotiating with other people, becoming a public figure, and *selling* your products and services to the world. There is a level of discomfort for a lot of people in this world when it comes to the activity of **negotiating** either for a salary, a product price, or a service cost, but also, when trying to persuade others, or trying to influence others towards **buying** your products, services o ideas.

Let's say **for example** that one day, you were walking down the streets, and you saw the girl of your dreams, but you were afraid of talking to her. Or if you are a girl and saw the boy of your dreams but you were hesitant to talk to him, because you thought he might see you as too pushy. The truth is that, **if** either one of these individuals, do not pass their level of **discomfort** to go and talk to the other person, that relationship might never develop or foster, for neither one of them, if none of them start a **conversation**. If fear of rejection is what is holding you back, you will never reach your **objective**. And objectives can only be measured by **results.** You will have to confront your fears in order for you to obtain or achieve your goals and results. Or you will have to **confront** your comfort zones if you truly want to achieve extraordinary things. And that goes for everything in life. In that sense, please do go and follow your dreams, reach for the stars and **conquer your fears.** Do go and achieve those things that you never thought you could do. Have a leap of faith in yourself, and you will see, all the beautiful things that you might be missing out in life. Also, remember, once you are an **expert on any field**, you level of discomfort diminishes, and your level of confidence and comfort increases. Therefore, if you become excellent at any practice, you won't have to worry anymore about living outside of your comfort zone, because what it is today your discomfort zone, will be your comfort zone tomorrow. Remember, practice makes perfect. Also, always stick to the law, when it comes to achieving greatness.

Making Others Uncomfortable

Although this is a *practice* that I do not recommend for you to use everywhere, or in every type of situations, the act of making others uncomfortable, can be observed as a good tactic, when it comes to the art of *negotiation.* Therefore, this is a practice that you should know and maybe at some point in time (not every time) *apply* when the situation *demands* it. The truth is that we as human beings or as individuals like to minimize our discomfort levels and *maximize* our comfort zones. We strive to be happy, and for those reasons, a good portion of humanity tend to be people pleasing, in order to avoid conflict, and reduce the risk of a fight, or a discussion to happen or develop. But the truth is that, when it comes to the art of *negotiating*, whether if it is in business, family matters, diplomacy, and politics, there will always be a *trade-off,* between the outcome that you want from that negotiation process, and the outcome that the other party wants from that negotiation process. And the truth is that if you go to that *negotiation table,* without being able to get outside of your comfort zone, you might end up giving away everything that you have ever worked for or owned, to the other party. Think of a *divorce settlement*. You have to be very careful in these types of situations. In other words, if you want to win that negotiation process, you will have to make other people *uncomfortable.*

For those reasons, you do not go to the negotiation table, trying to give all your assets away, but on the contrary, you go to the negotiation table wanting *to keep* all your assets for your self, and make sure that the other person is uncomfortable, or comfortable depending on the situation or outcome that you want to see. Within the sales world, for example, a good portion of the cold calling and outbound sales channels is all about making other people *uncomfortable*. It is all about disrupting other's people lives in order to offer them things, product or services that they might not want or need, but just because you as a salesperson **push them** on their pain points and trigger on their level of discomfort, they bought your product just so that you could go away.

Think of it as **peer pressure** system. How many times in life, have you done things in life, just because all your friends or colleagues **pushed you** into it. You acted, to satisfy their demands because your friends or colleagues put you in a very uncomfortable situation, where you were not strong enough to **say no** to them, but you simply felt a victim of their **pressure** and their demands. If you were confident enough to **say no,** then you **reverse** that pressure on to them. But if you said yes, you fall victim of the pressure of others on **to you** to do or buy things. Remember, as Warren Buffett says, "The Difference between Successful people and **really successful** people is that successful people say no to almost everything."

You can imagine, these acts of **peer pressure**, multiplying as more people show up, and they all begin to add pressure on to your life. If you are **confident** enough, and you can live past that discomfort zone of having all of them, telling you to do something, and you **say no**, then you have conquered your self-confidence, and become a **leader** to them instead. But if you always fall onto the demands or needs of others, you will forever become a victim of not being able to live outside of your comfort zone, by being a people pleaser all your life. Therefore, at some point in life, you will have to learn how to **say no**, when there is no benefit for you. And that responsibility increases a lot when you are a millionaire, or when you are a business owner. You cannot go outside in the business world, or begin the process of **wealth creation** or management, trying to please everybody. On the contrary, you will have to *reverse* that pressure on to others so that you can obtain a win from that negotiation table.

Try to become Free from Prejudice.

The market place is full of a *diverse* pool of people, with multiple needs, identities, personalities, and stages in life. There are multiple races, cultures, and traditions, just like there are multiple languages and different personal lifestyles. Therefore, it is important that you as a "Business Person" leave all the differences aside, and focus more on the wealth creation process. Making sure that all your products and services are sold to *the greatest* amount of people. Yes, I know, we talked about focusing on niche markets when it comes to an effective marketing and selling process. But at the same time, always remember, that it is better to be inclusive, when selling, rather than exclusive. Yes, of course, you can sell *the idea of exclusivity* for a lot of your products and add value to them, but the truth is that you want the largest amount of people to buy your products and services at the end. For those reasons, you have to become flexible and adaptable in the market place. Be *willing to sell* to everyone. Sell them at least *the idea* of buying your products. If they can afford your products right now, maybe someday they will, so, therefore, try to *appeal* to the largest amount of people when it comes to selling your products.

Leverage Other People's Skills – The Art Of Managing Human Resources

Talking about being uncomfortable, how about the activity of *managing* others. Does it make you uncomfortable, or you are a master at this practice? The truth is that this could be considered as one of the most difficult positions to be in, because of all the unique **challenges** that being a leader in a corporate environment might bring to you as an individual and as a business manager. But the truth is that **somebody** has to do the job, and what better person to lead a group of employees and to achieve the mission and goals of a company than **yourself**. Because the truth is that if you are an organized person who strives for richness and wealth, but you are also disciplined and a personal example from a lot of people around you in the practice of managing others, this activity should also become second **nature to you**.

The truth is that leadership **is not cheap**, and companies but also, the military regimes, and governments across **the world** know this. **Leadership is expensive**, and that is the bottom line. For those reasons, it is not only critical that you know or learn how to manage your **capital resources** effectively but also that you learn how to manage your **human resources** in effective ways.

In order for you to leverage your employees, to **make money** for your business or company, you need to learn how to take advantage of these resources and manage them in the best possible ways. Remember that, **leverage** means obtaining maximum productivity with minimum effort. In other words, have your money, and your employees make money for you, with little optimized and organized effort. Also, make no mistake. If you are the owner of the company; your employees are there also to help you **make money**. You pay them a salary, in exchange for their time, but it is their duty to help you make money and get your business running properly. Otherwise, you can and should *fire them*.

My Employee Experience:

In my experience as an employee a long time ago, I learned that those who hire me and give me a job, not only have *authority* over me in the *job place* but also they deserve to make an income out of my services; if and when they *hire me*. I do not have the right, just to be a *business expense* to them, but on the other hand, I have to offer a return of investment to my employers. If I do not bring any return of investment to my employer, then he or she should fire me as a *consequence*.

In fact, I also believe that so long as I am happy and satisfied with the amount of money my bosses are paying me, then, there should be no issue with them, making money out of *my time and resources*, if I am happy with what they are *paying* me. The fact is that the main focus of every Business owner or manager is to make money for its company. Except, for the non-for-profit corporations of course. Therefore, I could no get mad, if companies were trying to make money *out of me,* because I know that is the nature of the beast.

A long time ago, for instance, I discovered that a few companies that I worked for in the past, before becoming an *entrepreneur*, were trying to take a cut, out of my hourly salary for them.

To give you a clear example, *company A*, a company that I worked for in the past, was paying $40 USD for a position (x) in their company. But for some reason, company A was not able to hire anybody on time to fulfill that role. Therefore, *Company A* hired *Company B* to find a qualified employee for them. *Company B* found the qualified candidate for *Company A*, but they offered the employee a $30 USD per hour salary for that same position (x). That employee was myself, and I agreed to that salary. *Company B* was paying me $30 US dollars per hour, and they were making $10 US dollars out of every hour I worked for *Company A* because *Company A* was paying to *Company B* $40 USD for my services as mentioned before.

This was a decent chunk of my hour salary over time, but I had no idea this was happening until *"Company A"* decided to hire me directly. They disclosed all the information to me, everything that had happened with *Company B*, and that is how I learned that *Company B* had taken a good portion of my salary over a long period of time while they acted as the *middleman* between me and *company A*. That is what *leveraging* other people's skills and time means in the *human resources* agency world. And I see this happening everywhere in the market place.

My Entrepreneurial Experience:

The other day, a good *colleague* of mine, with whom I worked in the film industry during my early years, told me that he pays $150 USD dollars per day to his employees, while he charges $250 USD for them in the Budget he presented to the film production agency. Therefore, he is making $100 profit out of every employee he uses for his film project every day.

Therefore, this is a scenario that happens everywhere, and if the employee agrees with it, I don't see a problem with this scenario, because chances are that the person acting as the **middleman**, had the skills to find a job for someone else, and they should be rewarded for that process as well. Meaning if I find you a job, and you are happy with it, and you are happy with the money I offer you, then it does not matter whether if I am charging more, for your services to the other contracting company in order to make some profit out of you. That is what is called leverage. If you and I are happy with our deal, then we are conducting **good business.** Of course, you as the employee could get upset, when you discover this practice, especially if you discover that other employees and colleagues are getting paid much better than you are for the same job.

Another good friend of mine, for instance, has a company that provides swimming pool lifesaver services to a lot of buildings in New York City. He pays $15 USD dollars per hour to his lifesavers but charges $20 USD to the buildings for each hour one of his lifesavers is working for them. In that sense, he makes a lot of money out of the more than **50 lifesavers** that he has working for him. At a full-time rate, he makes $2000 USD a day out of the 50 lifesavers working for him. Not bad for a business model. That is also. Leveraging your employees.

Another example could be a **television casting company**, that pays $50 USD, to every television extra they can get on a talk show, but their company receives $100 US dollars, out of every television extra they get to that show. In a way, that is a human resource **leverage** middleman business model that can work well for a lot of people.

You can also see a lot of these business processes within the *schools* and other *training* development companies. A good friend of mine who has an excellent dancing school in the city of New York also told me a little bit about this business model. He makes money out the students, paying for tuition, but he also makes a lot of money out of the contracts he gets for his exceptional dancers, to go out and travel the world doing fantastic performances. He only pays his dancers; however, *half* of what the company that hires his company offers him for his dancers.

If company A hires his dance company to create a dance performance for a period of six months, and in the process Company A pays $300 USD per dancer per day, he only pays his dancers $200 USD per day. Of course, you have to account all the other business operations expenses that his business may carry in order to keep his business afloat, but overall, these are all acts tactics of *leveraging* other people's talent and time in order to make money out of them. You can definitely see this type of business model being *replicated* all around the world. You could even replicate in your business if you follow all the legal rules and comply with your local and federal laws to make additional income for your business.

In that sense, you have to be like John D. Rockefeller. He used to say the following, "I have ways of making money that you know nothing of." A lot of your employees and students will be thrilled to have you finding them a job, or giving them a job.

They do not need, to know, that you might be charging them a *recurring fee*, for finding them that job. This is a business model that could be considered as useful when managing large quantities of employees or student who are looking for jobs. Of course, when you respect the law in the process.

Also, in order to close this chapter, just acknowledge that principle number six of this book is to *"leverage other people's resources and time."* You don't always have to use your own money and resources to achieve your business goals. Sometimes all you have to do is leveraging other's people time and resources to achieve economic success.

Principle # 6
Leverage other people's skills and resources

Chapter 7:

Take the Stage

According to Dan Lok, a self-made millionaire and marketing Guru who has made tons and tons of money via his Youtube.com channel, *"Stage time is wealth time"* and I could not agree more with him on that single statement. Because at the end, what *the stage* does, at any given point in time, is to give you *exposure* of you and your brand and products or services, to a larger *audience* that is willing and able to hear your story or talent, knowledge and skills, but also, that is willing *to buy* your products and services, if you end up appealing to them in a positive and constructive way. Think of it as a *marketing message* that you present to the largest amount of people or audience as possible in a single room or space, where you have all their entire attention, and you can influence them and their emotions, towards *connecting* with you while building a lasting relationship with you that could make them buy your products and services right there and then, *on the spot.*

That is the reason why stage time is so *valuable*. Because it maximizes the exposure of your message to a *large* number of people or audience, where you can and will have *an influential* voice over them, to guide them or drive them into your message, while obtaining the outcome that you desire from that interaction at that point in time.

The key when taking the stage is to utilize that exposure time, to build *credibility* for your self or your persona, your character, and your products so that people can *trust you*. When you have earned the people's trust, then, by all means, it will be a lot easier for you to sell your products, knowledge or talent to them and the entire world. For those, and multiple other reasons, stage time is *wealth time*, because via the use of the stage, people will be able to see or identify *who* you really are as a person, but also what is it that you are offering to them, and whether or not they can *connect* with you and your message in ways that they never did before.

Why do you think that some of the highest paid well-known Hollywood actors charge millions and *millions of dollars*, for participating in a single movie? First of all, because, people *love* them and *trust* them as actors, but also, because they have obtained the *fame* and *earned* the credibility that their previous stage performances have given to them. People *trust them* as good actors, but also, people recognize them, as talented, influential people in the entertainment world, who can truly *immerse* you as an audience into their characters or movie settings.

The same goes for some of the most influential music artists from around the world, who can become millionaires simply by conducting a well-known tour of *concerts* around the world. For these amazing music artist stage time is not only wealth time in terms of future business opportunities and possibilities, but it is also wealth time that is received at the moment that millions and *millions of people* pay to go to see their concerts and see them performing the music that has put these musicians in these privileged places in the first place. The more people that go to your events and *pay to see you*, the more money you will be able to make in one single concert, or stage performance. Tell me if that is not *wealth time*.

According to Forbes Magazine, just to give you an example, Ed Sheeran is the artist that had the most profitable tour of 2018:

> His tour *"Divide*," "which isn't over yet, grossed an eye-popping $429 million in 2018 alone, according to *Billboard*. That sum is astounding, and one of the largest showings ever, but it doesn't even tell the whole story. Sheeran started the tour that supports his latest blockbuster album ÷ (*Divide*) in 2017, and in that year, it was able to rack up well over *$100 million* in ticket sales. The British singer-songwriter still has dozens of shows scheduled, and it's likely he'll end up on this same last when it is compiled at the end of 2019, possibly with over $100 million *more* tacked on to the tour's total". [17] *(Source Forbes Magazine)*

How about that kind of revenue for a music tour; *impressive right?* Tell me if stage time has not meant wealth creation time for *Ed Sheeran* between 2017 and 2019. Of course, he has increased his wealth by a couple of hundreds of million dollars, after all his tour's operation cost is accounted for. Therefore, stage time means a lot of money for him, seriously speaking.

Tony Robbins, for instance, one of the most influential motivational coaches of all times, has also made a significant amount of money and impact in the world due to his *stage time*, because, at the end, stage time mans *credibility* time. People know him as one of the most influential motivators from all over the world, as he has been able to change the lives of thousands and thousands of people who have assisted to his events. In that sense, stage time is also wealth creation time for Tony Robbins every time somebody goes to his motivational speaker events.

The truth is that if you want to attend one of Tony Robbins conferences in 2019 you will have to pay $56 USD for the cheapest ticket, multiplied by 50 thousand people who will attend one of his conferences, and that is a lot of money. That is $2.800,000,00 USD to be more precise, *just for one big conference*. Think about how much money is left for him after operational expenses in one single event, and that is a lot of money.

But of course, being at the center of the stage is not enough to build money, capital, fame or credibility. You have to *deliver value* to your audience, depending on what type of knowledge or entertainment is that you are offering to them. The bottom line is that you have to *deliver* a good message when you get to the stage. You have got to be *persuasive* in your message. And you have got to influence your audience to buy your products and services. The truth is that you want them to see you as a *credible* and reliable source of entertainment or knowledge in the market place.

Grab the Microphone

Audience size matters of course. But at the end, the most important thing you can do, regardless of your audience size, is grabbing the *microphone*. Because the reality is that when you are grabbing the microphone, you are grabbing people's *attention*, but you are also grabbing *control* of the stage and your audience. You can tell your audience to do almost anything you want them to do, and they are very likely to follow because at the end, concerts and conferences are *controlled* environments where people usually do what the person with the microphone tells them or suggests them to do.

When you are in control of the *microphone*, you are in control of the *discussion*, or at the very least, you can influence the conversation towards the topics or themes that you want to debate or discuss. Of course, the level of impact you are going to have varies on the type of stage you are performing in, but it will always be vital for you to *grab* the microphone if you want to influence those who are or will be listening to you.

The truth is that the microphone is *your friend* in the wealth creation process because it amplifies your voice so that everyone around you can hear you. In that sense, go ahead and grab the microphone where and whenever you can, and if you can add a *call to action* to that message that you are delivering with the microphone, by all means do it, because remember, people are very likely to follow your directions when you have the microphone, so *take advantage* of that.

Another critical element to remember when taking the stage is that "Public Speaking" is *high-income* money making skill. When you learn to speak to the public in eloquent ways, your audience and your credibility increases in multiple ways, but also the level of *influence* you have over others in your immediate environment. Therefore, public speaking is a very important skill to *develop*, if you want to be wealthy, because the more and the better that you can speak to the masses, the more income that you are likely to obtain in return. In that sense, if you can invest in *your voice*, and your speech delivery process, you are very likely to *multiply* your sources of income and influence in ways that you never thought possible before.

Deliver a Dramatic Experience

People *love* experiences, and they also love good *storytelling*. But it is not always easy to grab people's attention right away. For those reasons, the very same Tony Robbins always says that you must begin any type of speech, or message delivery process, by sharing with people a *dramatic* experience in order to grab their *attention right away*. For example, "When I was writing my first book I was dirt poor, and living in my car, but now I am a multimillionaire, living in a Mansion in Miami Beach due to my newly learned money making skills." How is that for a dramatic experience?

The truth is that dramatic experiences grab people's attention, but also people will always need to have a *wow factor*, every time they come to see you, because, at the end, these types of experiences do sell, but also, because, a lot of people are going through some dramatic experiences on their own, and they can *connect* with you right away, in empathic ways when you share these types of experiences with them.

The truth is that people give a lot of value to *a good experience*, and they pay big money for those reasons. That is the reason you go to a *Five Star Hotel*, in order to live that experience. Or you go to *Disneyworld* in order to live the experience with your kids. Or you go to vacations on the beach, to live that experience, because experiences do matter.

The reality is that experiences have a lot of value in the market place, so when people go to see you, whether if it is at a concert venue or movie theater, make sure that they have a *valuable* and good experience that is going to leave them with a *smile* on their faces and the *wow factor* across their minds. If you are able to deliver a good experience for your audiences, chances are that your clients or customers are going to be happy, and they are going to **recommend** your conferences, concerts and other events, to other people, so that they can come to see your act and experience what you have **shared** with them.

Also the more **interactive** that your events are; the better the experience your customers will have. Therefore, make sure that your customers or audience are **engaged** in the process and that they **participate** everywhere they can in your event. Have your audience engaged with questions, funny games, dances, and other interactive method and mechanisms. They will appreciate you for that effort. Also, try to create **an energy** of celebration in your event and multiply it, if that is your aim with your speech. If you are trying to **motivate** your audience and making them happy, that is an excellent way to make it happen. The goal here is to try to have your audience forget about the outside world, but also make sure that you give them good value and return of investment for visiting you. They will reward you for that over the long and short-term period of time, by promoting you and your brand with their friends and acquaintances for future reference and events.

Type of Stages

The **types of stages** also do matters when it comes to obtaining value and recognition for your message or speech, depending on where you are delivering that message. It is not the same to deliver a speech to your classmates in the classroom, than delivering a speech at a Ted Talk, or at an **Oscar or Grammy** award ceremony. The truth is that the stage where you deliver your message also, carries a level of recognition and **legitimacy** for others, in the outside world. For those reasons, do think about the type of stage where you are delivering your message, but always remember, in today's day and age, that the most important thing is to deliver the message. Chances are that if the message is good, funny or entertaining, or helpful, it will become *viral* in the social media channels, and maybe, have the massive impact that you want your message to have in the social media world. In that sense, always focus on your *message first*, because at the end, if the message is the correct one, the bigger platform or stage will eventually show up and be offered to you, once people begin to listen to you and recognize in mass quantities for your message or talent that you are offering to them.

If you are at the beginning stages of *public speaking*, for motivation speaking purposes, a *"Ted Talk"* platform can be a great avenue to give your stage time with value and credibility. Just remember principle number seven of this books when delivering that message, which says, *stage time is wealth time*, and you will make sure that you make the best out of that stage time, whether that stage experience might be.

Principle # 7
Stage Time Is Wealth Time

Chapter 8

Money is energy

Everything in life if you think very hard about it is *energy*. At the end, everything is composed of atoms, that have unique characteristics and attributes that make them act in certain ways when dealing with the laws of physics, but at the end, everything in life is energy. Most importantly, for the purposes of this book, *money* is also energy.

Energy by definition means, "the capacity (ability) or power *to do work*, such as the capacity to move an object (of a given mass) by the application of force. Energy can exist in a variety of forms, such as electrical, mechanical, chemical, thermal, or nuclear, and can be transformed from one form to another"[18]. Therefore, if you really think about it, money *is also* the capacity to *do work* at the human level, because by the means of money, you can have most of the people of the world doing work for you, and moving objects for you, or creating new products, projects, services, technologies or innovative ideas for you. Because the truth is that *money moves* the world, at least for all of us human beings. Money is what makes all of *us work*, and money is a tool, to achieve things that otherwise, it would be impossible for us to achieve. Therefore, money *is like energy*, in economic terms, but also, in terms of social activity and capacity. The more money that you have; the more work that you will be able to do, or get done on your behalf, but also the more *influence* or hire capacity that you will have over other people to perform work for you.

There is also *kinetic* energy and *potential* energy. Kinetic energy is energy in *motion*, kind of like a motorcycle, or a car moving in the road, or your *body* moving at will. In that sense, kinetic energy requires movement, action, activity and it usually builds *momentum*, because kinetic energy is energy *at work* — meaning; energy that is actively in motion, time and space. Of course, in the large scale of things, *everything* in the universe seems to be in motion, but within the context of our *planet earth*, some things are moving faster in relation to others, and that is just the ultimate truth.

Think about the relationship between a mountain and the wind. Which one of those two elements moves faster? The wind is in *constant motion*, therefore producing kinetic energy, and the mountain is standing still, in relationship to the wind. Of course, in the large scale of things in the universe, *everything* is in motion, even that mountain, which moves with the rotation of the earth in space. But the wind, in contrast to the mountain, moves a lot faster, when you observe it from the Mountain Top. It is very difficult to explain, but *Einstein's* theory of *relativity* applies in this equation.

Just to explain a little further "the theory of relativity states that objects will move slower and shorten in length from the *point of view* of an *observer* on Earth. [19]. Therefore, in order to explain my case, if you look at the earth from a space shuttle, the earth is moving along with *everything* inside the planet. But if you are on *top of a mountain*, the mountain according to your perception is not moving, but the *wind* is.

Therefore, your perception of movement is relative to your point of view in time and space.

But back to the **topics of money,** in economic and investment terms, kinetic energy could be represented, by the activity of having your **money in motion** actively **working for you.** Similar to a cash flow **investment** that is producing a cash return on your investment right away. Meaning your money is **actively working** for you. Think of it, like compound interest, a Money lending instrument that puts your money to work right away and is actively bringing a return of investment for you.

Potential energy, on the other hand, is like having a **savings** account in investment terms. Potential energy is energy that is **being stored** but also **lacks** movement. Kind of like a big rock that is not moving, it is energy that is being safeguarded and stored in a body of mass that is not moving. This type of energy is not producing activity, motion, or building momentum, but is getting stored in a storage space, or in financial terms, in your **bank account**. Is like money that you have in your **savings account** that is not producing any return of investment, or additional money for you. It has the potential to make money for you but is not making any money right now at this point in time, because this money is **not active** and you are just saving it for a later date.

In that sense, you can see that there is a straightforward relationship between money and energy. **Money is energy**, and you should be able to secure it, maintain it, manage it, multiply it or accumulate it for your future activities and life projects. The **more money** you have, the more work or influence over others that you will have. But also, the more **energy** you will have in your life, overall.

Think about how happy or energized you feel when you get your *paycheck*, or when you get money from someone else. You become so excited, nobody can remove that happiness away from you. Because money is literally like an *energy shot* that is given to you that allows you to do things that otherwise you would not be able to do. The truth is that just like anything else in this world, we as human beings are also energy, but so it is the money that we use to exchange for our products, services and time. When we hire somebody else to do a job for us, we are hiring their *time and energy* to work for us. In a way, a money transfer is like a *transfer of energy*. A mechanism to get a person rewarded for the use of their energy.

But if you work for free, that other person is taking that energy away from you. That is why you should *never* work for free. You have to change your mentality towards money, and how you use your time and begin to consider it as a source of energy for your life and your goals in life. Do not give your time and energy away for free. *It is very valuable.* Make sure that you charge *a lot* of money for it in return.

They say that money is not everything in life, which might be accurate, but the truth is that you will definitely be able to conduct a lot more work and get more stuff done when you have an *abundance* of money in your bank account. Think about a family member of you being in the hospital. It is only money, what in today's day and age, will buy them the *proper care*, that will assure you the best quality of service for your family member. If your family member does not have a good insurance, or can't pay for the hospital, then chances are that the nurses and doctors at the hospital will not give that person good care, just because nobody will pay for the service or the bill that is being charged to that patient.

The reality is that the business world, just like in a war zone, is a *realist* world, where people demand something in exchange for their time and services. People are not willing to give up their time for free, and *neither* should you. So the activity of accumulating wealth is a very realistic and pragmatic act, of improving your quality of life, but also, of enhancing your ability to do work in your society and across the world. Without money, traveling to China from the U.S will be a lot harder, than when you have money, and that goes for every business transaction in the market place.

That is why, the activity of making money is so important in life, especially after you become older and realize that money is the most *effective tool* in today's world to achieve your goals and needs. If you do not have the ability to make a lot of money, you will lack the resources to live in a comfortable and abundant life. You will not be able to pay for the life insurance of your kids or other family members.

For those reasons, your money is like your *energy*. You have to try to foster it, nurture and multiply it. Take care of it like a precious metal and don't just waste it. The more money you have, the more energy you will have in the market place.

Therefore, the act of investing and multiplying your money is crucial. Just like taking care of a *plant*, you must safeguard your money, but also, nurture it to make it grow. You can nurture it properly by taking good care of it. By treating it like a baby, that is one day going to grow old and become prosperous and successful. In that sense, you have to *create the conditions* for your money to grow, because the reality is that money, will give you things that only a lot of money can give you, such as economic comfort and abundance, but only if you *treat it right*, just like any other thing in life. Money is energy, and as such you have got to handle it. Money can give you all the power you need to achieve your goals and dreams. Therefore, you have got to **attract it.**

Also remember, it takes time to accumulate wealth. Therefore, save your money, nurture it, mature it, take good care of it and multiply it. As Warren Buffett says, "Somebody is sitting in the shade today because somebody planted a tree a long time ago." Plant your **tree of wealth** and let it grow over time.

Don't Give Your Energy Away

Why do you think that energy is so expensive in today's market place? Because energy moves the world. Think about the oil market and how much you have been paying for the use of gas over the past few years. If you filled up your fuel tank once a week for a $35 USD value, you would have spent $1680 USD a year, just in gas money. In that sense, energy is expensive, and gas is not given away for free. You have to **pay for it.**

So why is it that you are giving away your energy for free? Why is it that you work for free? Why is it that you are giving free consultations? The truth is that there are **energy vampires** out there who you have to be on the lookout for, and the first thing they will do is try to take your energy away from you by **not paying** you correctly for your time, effort services, and expertise.

Don't allow for that to happen. Don't give your energy away for free. Charge for your time, as if you were valuable enough to earn that money in exchange. For example, I know some people, whose **One Hour Consultation Fee** is valued at $10,000.00 USD. Why should you not value your hours at the same price? Remember, you are worth it. Therefore, **don't give** any of your hours for free.

If there is not any return of investment for your time, you will be losing your time, your money and your energy in the process. Make sure that other people *value your time* and effort in economic terms, where they know that every one of your hours is worth a lot of money and that in exchange for your time and energy, you will need a lot of money in *return*. Remember, money is energy, and the more you have of it, the better you will be over time. *Charge accordingly.*

In that respect, the *rule number one* of this chapter is to not give away your energy for free, and *rule number two* is always charge for your time and effort accordingly. *Rule number three* is not forgetting rule number 1 and 2. *Never* give your energy away, and always charge for your time and effort. *Make sure* that people *pay you well* for your time and energy.

Principle #8
Money is Energy. Never give your energy away for free.

Chapter 9

Produce More Than You Consume

Principle # 9
Producing is better than Consuming

I know; we have been programmed to consume. From every angle at a very early age, all we do is *consume*. We buy, buy, buy and consume, even things that we don't need. And that is fine, but the truth is that it is a lot better to be on the *producer side*, than on the consumer side, in the market place.

Processes of creativity and innovation drive the production of new products and services in our minds and environments. Therefore, it is a lot more rewarding for *the brain*, but also, for *the producer*, when his products and services *are sold* in the world. But the production of products and services can also come at a higher cost. Therefore, you will have to keep in mind principle number three of this book, which is to *keep your cost down*, especially when it comes to manufacturing your products or services, but also, when taking care of your operational cost. In order for you to make a net income, which equals to revenue minus expenses, you will have *to keep your cost down*. In that sense, one of the most essential elements of a successful business strategy is to keep your cost low and making sure you make a *net income*, or profit in the process from the revenue your products and services are producing.

Of course, you can also put your self in the shoes of the **middleman** in order to make a lot of money. The middleman buys from the manufacturer or producer at a very low price and then sells to the consumer at a **higher price**. We talked about this activity as an effective money-making tactic or strategy, in the principle number one of this book; which teaches you to **buy low and sell high** any type of product or service in the market place with the aim of making a profit out of it. This practice can also be understood as a **capital gains** type of investment. This could be a brilliant strategy if you want to save your self from the hustle of the manufacturing or production process, and you want to make money out of the **selling process** instead.

However, under most circumstances, it is always better to be on the producer side, than on the consumer side. Because being on the producer side, gives you a **greater margin for profit**, and capital gains, but also greater control about what product or service you want to see in the world. Think about Jeff Bezos. How much money do you think it cost him to create Amazon.com? The truth is that for Jeff Bezos, his initial investment was of $300,000,00 USD, obtained from a loan from his parents. But look where his company is right now, making $233 Billion dollars only during the fiscal year 2018. That is a lot of money in the pockets of Jeff Bezos, from an initial 300 thousand dollar investment. He is a billionaire now, and the wealthiest person in the world. For those reasons, it is always a lot better to have a producer mentality than a consumer mentality. Being a producer of a marvelous product can be the lottery ticket that will make you become a millionaire, or Billionaire, if you develop the right platform, product or service, at the right point in time.

Because at the end, it is always better to be on the creative side, at least you won't have any regrets when you see your products and services becoming a reality. You will be proud of your own creations, and that in itself will make you proud and happy. Yes, we are all creative human beings, and it just a matter of creating products or services that you are passionate about, in order to obtain success.

That is why, I recommend to you that if you love cars and mechanics and you are given a $30000.00 Budget to buy a car, build your own car, with your own brand and identity. Or, if you love fashion and you can use the sewing machine, instead of buying clothes, make your own clothes. If people love them, they will buy them from you. And if you are a musician, create your own music. Don't; just sing covers, but make your own creations. Just make sure that your own products, have your own identity and authenticity in them. People value authenticity. Therefore, go ahead, be creative and believe in your self. Don't just buy products that already exist out there.

If you are a Chef, make your signature dish and develop your own recipes and restaurants. Don't be afraid of creating, innovating and developing your own companies and your own sources of income based on your own authentic products and services.

First of all, start by believing in your self, your identity, and your authenticity. You are a magical creative box, but at the end, it is only you who can unleash that creativeness, and offer productivity and value to the market place.

Also, when producing your own products or services, always remember to keep your production cost low. Think about Antonio Banderas and some of the Hollywood Movies where he has participated so far. Some of his movies have made millions and millions of dollars, and others have lost millions and millions of dollars. The big differences between these financial results is that a lot of the movies where he participated that made millions of dollars, were produced at a **low cost**. In other words, they kept the cost low. Think about the Movie Trilogy that derives from the movie "El Mariachi." "El Mariachi," "Desperado" and "Once Upon a Time in Mexico" were a set of three films that were directed by Robert Rodriguez, were Antonio Banderas was the protagonist of the movies. The movie "El Mariachi," for example, was a movie that was produced with a $7000.00 USD budget and made a profit of two million dollars. How is that for a profit? That is a 286 X profit margin. Their initial investment of $7000.00 USD, multiplied itself by 286, making them a $2,000,000.00 dollars in the process.

The second movie from this trilogy, *"Desperado"* for example, was produced with a $7 million dollar budget and grossed over $24.6 million in U.S theaters. That is a 17.6 Million dollar profit just within the U.S. And the third movie from this trilogy, *"Once Upon a Time in Mexico"* was made for $29 million and grossed over $56.3 million domestically and an additional $41.8 million worldwide. That is a total of a 69.1 Million dollar profit out of one single movie. Just in theater tickets sales, of course. These values do not account for other sales avenues for these movie productions may have obtained via media sales in other television network providers such as HBO.

On the opposite side of the coin, however, Antonio Bandera's movie "the 13th Warrior" which was directed by John McTiernan, lost 100 million dollars after all numbers were plotted and accounted for. This movie was produced with a $161 US million dollars budget but ended up making only $61US million dollars in the box office. That is a significant loss of 100 million dollars in one single movie. Again, the big difference here was the production cost. Therefore, always remember, to keep your production cost low. The lower the cost of your production, the higher the margin for profit or gain.

Produce Digital Products

In today's digital age, there are a lot more products and services that can be produced at a lower cost, in the digital format, than on any other non-digital channel. Think about books and e-books, training webinars, online courses, digital photos, and so on. You can relatively produce these type of products on a digital format, and sell them online without accounting too much for manufacturing cost, but of course, adding a good marketing strategy to them. Because as we mentioned before, it does not matter what type of product or service you have created, you will always have to market it appropriately. If you do not use an effective marketing strategy, like the ones we mention in chapter four of his book, you will never be able to sell your products or services.

What you can do, however, is to minimize production cost, by creating products and services that require low cost and low maintenance. For those reasons, digital products and even digital store fronts, are the most cost-effective than non-digital products or stores. The key here is to drive traffic to your products or storefronts, which in the digital world, can be obtained from developing an excellent digital marketing strategy. Always remember, keep your cost down, and profit high.

The bottom line is that it is a lot better for you to stay on the production side, instead of the consumption side, when it comes to making money and becoming a millionaire. If you purposefully stay on the producer side rather than on the consumer side, chances are that you will one day, develop, produce or manufacture a product or service that one-day could or will make you a millionaire. Think of it like a lottery ticket. The more products that you develop, the more chances that one day, one of those products will make you a millionaire. Also remember to visit my online store, www.fabianavilastore.com. You will find al my books, music and services at this website.

Chapter 10

Time is Money

Unfortunately, we don't really value time too much, until it begins to become a **limited resource**, as we grow old. It is only then when we begin to appreciate time a lot more and to think about how we spend it properly, and how much more **value** we get from it, in a way that we never did or think before. Because the truth is that **time**, is one of the most valuable assets that we have in our lives. Therefore, we must value it, foster it, and spend it wisely, but also, make a lot of **money** out of it. Therefore, instead of regretting not having used our time properly in the past, let's focus on how we can use our time properly now, **from now on**, moving forward, especially when it comes to implementing a wealth creation or management strategy inside our minds and our companies.

Every second of your life counts, but also, every activity that you do with it. Therefore, just like money should be **well invested** in the things that are going to give you a positive return on investment in the future, **time** should also be well invested. That is why, often when you are near the end of your high school program, a lot of your financial, accounting or mathematics professors begin to tell you to **save** your money or **invest** it properly. Because chances are that **if** you begin to **save** your money, or you begin to put $200 dollars a month in a personal retirement account, from the age of 20, at a rate of return of 10%, it is very likely that you will end up with a total of $2,096,646.00 U.S. dollars by the age of 65. It could be a little more or a little less, depending on what type of investment vehicle you use and also the rate of return you negotiate when you begin the process of saving. However, most likely, the outcome of your $200 USD per month investment; is that you will end up with a little bit more than $2,000.000.00 U.S. dollars by the age of 65 in your **bank account.** That is a lot of **money** for some people, especially those who will be old and out of work by the age of 65.

My question to you is the following: would you rather have $2,132,467.00 U.S. dollars in your **bank account** by the age of 65 or would you rather have $0 dollars in your bank account by the age of 65? I hope you think like a millionaire, and like the $2,132,467.00 number.

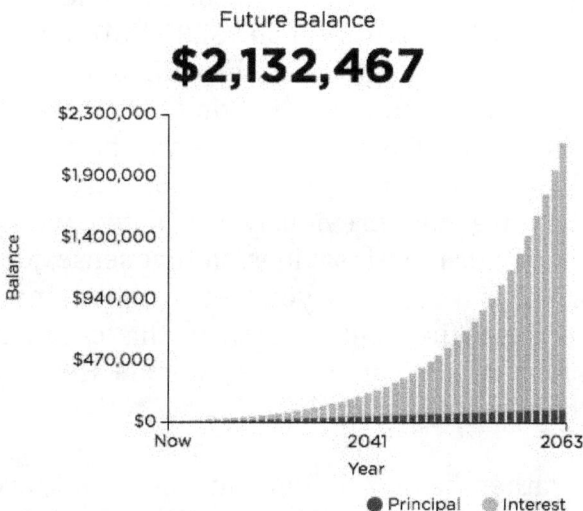

Future Balance

$2,132,467

Fig. 1 –Returns $200 USD a month savings, over time with Compound Interest.

For those reasons we **encourage** everyone, especially young people to save their money, and **learn** about capital investment strategies and tactics from a very early age. Because the more knowledge you have about capital investment, the more likely that you are going to **become a millionaire** over time, but also the more likely that you will **keep and multiply** those millions.

Let's say that **you** were that same **little kid** who began to save $200 U.S dollars per month from the age of twenty. Let's say that you also enrolled in a **401K** when you first found your first job at the age of twenty. A 401K, for those who don't know, is a **workplace retirement** account. Let's say that the 401K from your job **matched** your $200 USD savings per month for your retirement account. (By the way, the process of matching in a 401k, means, that the company you work for, puts **the same** amount of money you are putting into your retirement account, **or** a small percentage of it, depending on your company's 401K terms). In this case, for example, let's say that your company's **401k** matched your $200 USD investment per month, meaning they added another $200 U.S dollars per month to your savings equation, making it a total of $400 USD per month. Because of that 401K **match**, you would end up with $4,247,255 US dollars by the age of 65, instead of the two million dollars we had previously calculated with only the $200 U.S dollars per month savings. In that sense, joining your workplace **401K** can duplicate your retirement money, just like it duplicated the retirement account in this case from a two million to a four million value in this example. How is that for a long-term retirement strategy?

Would you rather have 2 Million in your bank account, or would you rather have 4 million by the age of 65 on your retirement date? I hope the answer is 4 million.

Future Balance

$4,247,255

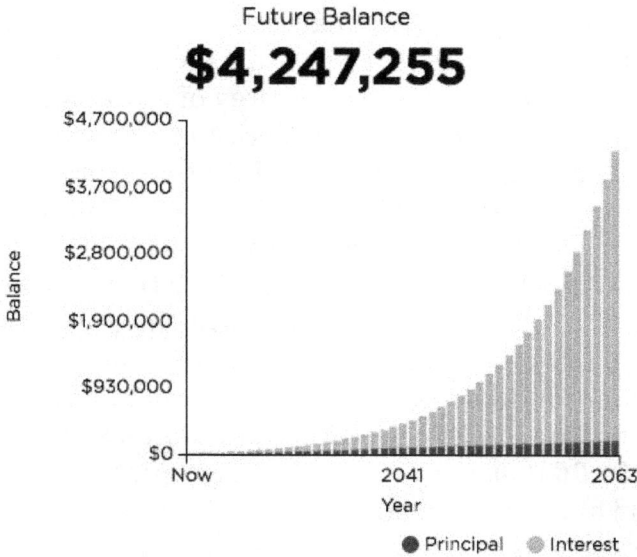

Fig 2 – Savings returns over time with Compound Interest and a 401K.

In that sense, we do encourage everyone who has a job to invest in these types of 401K retirement accounts, because at the end, not only you **must diversify** your investment portfolio, but also, you must invest in those long-term investment vehicles that are more **profitable** and secure for you. Of course, not everything is flowers and roses when it comes to the 401K accounts, so you must dive into the different 401K options that exist out there with a lot of care and analysis, to make sure you are making a safe and sound investment. But if you are a hard-working employee trying to multiply your retirement money in the workplace, make sure you use the **401K options** in your strategy to multiply your overall retirement's money.

In that sense, time does **rewards** economically to those who properly invest their money **wisely**. To give you another clear example about how much **"time"** can increase or multiply your money, let's look at the Apple Initial Public Offering (IPO), and how much money you would have made if you had purchased 20 shares of **Apple** back in 1980 when the company first went public. If you had purchased 20 shares of Apple Stock back in 1980, at the company's initial IPO price of $22 USD per share, you would have had to invest $440 USD from your capital. But after all the four stock splits and nearly 30 years later, you would own, or end up with approximately 1120 shares of Apple (AAPL). At a price of $997.55 USD per share as of November 2, 2018, you would have made a **profit** of $1,117,256 U.S dollars from your initial investment. That single investment of $440 dollars back in 1980 would have made you a **millionaire** in 38 years. **$440 dollars** turned into **$1,117,256.00** dollars in 38 years. Can you see the impact that time could have on your money?

When you invest your money correctly, on the right investment vehicles, at the right point in time, you will see the positive impact that **time** can have over the multiplication of your money. That is why we tell you to learn **to value your time**, not only in terms of how you experience life in itself but also, in terms of how you **invest** your money in life.

Time and Investing

There are four essential elements or variables that will always show up in a capital investment formula. **"Time and Timing"** are in fact, those kinds of elements that will always show up in the investment equation, in addition to **"Capital"** (money) of course. There is also one more variable that will always be present in any type of investment formula, and that is the variable of **"Where"** you want to invest your money for the formula to be complete. In other words, what type of investment vehicle you want to use. So in a way, these are the four *basic* elements for a reliable capital investment formula.

1) Capital	Money – How Much?
2) Time	How Long?
3) Timing	When?
4) Where	Investment Vehicle

In the previous Apple IPO example, for example, we determined that the **Capital** (how much money), we were going or invest was equal to $440 USD. We determined the **Timing** or (the when) we were going to invest, which was right at the IPO launch. We determine the **Time,** (how long) we were going to keep the investment, which was for 38 Year. And we determine the **Investment Vehicle** (where) we were going to invest our money, which was the **Apple** stock. Therefore, all those variables needed to be studied and accounted for, before making any type of investment capital decision. In this case, we did a good job.

Within the Real Estate industry for example, as we explained earlier in chapter one, time also adds value to your properties. A property that cost $200,000.00 in 2018 is very likely to increase in value over time to $220,000.00 by the year 2021, as time moves forward. The value increases at a rate that fluctuates depending on different variables such as inflation; supply and demand and other political pull and push factors.

When it comes to money lending, for example, *time* also adds value when capital Banks lend to the borrower over time with the **interest rate** they charge over the principal amount. If your bank lends you money under a contract with the use of **compound interest**, for example, they will be making a lot of money from you over the life of that loan, because compound interest is interest "calculated on the initial principal, which also includes all of the accumulated interest of previous periods of a deposit or loan. It can be thought of as *"interest on interest,"* and will make a sum of debt grow at a faster rate than simple interest, which is calculated only on the principal amount. The rate at which compound interest accrues depends on the frequency of compounding, such that the higher the number of compounding periods, the greater the compound interest"[19]. In that sense, be very careful when taking loans that may have compound interest in them. They might increase your debt over time to the point, where it will be challenging to pay them.

The truth is that time is *money,* whether if you want to believe it or not when it comes to your wealth creation or wealth portfolio management and investment process. Time is one of those *variables* that will always show up, in nearly every type of investment form, so pay attention to it.

Add Value to your Personal Time.

Let me ask you a straight up question. How much does your time costs? Or how much do you think your time costs? Have you ever asked your self that question? If someone asks you how much money does an hour of your life cost, what price would you put to it? Have you ever thought about that?

The answer you give to this question is critical for your life's value and your sense of *self-worth* in the market place. The more you value your time, the more, that others will value it and pay for it as you wish.

Think about the last visit to **the doctor** you did or **the dentist**. How much money did they charge you for their time? The truth is that they probably charged you or your insurance provider a lot of money, not only because they value their time, but also because you and our entire society, values their time. Of course, doctors do a great job when it comes to reducing or **removing** the **pains** and aches of our bodies, and doctors also work very well at making us a lot healthier with the use of their professional knowledge, treatments, and skills. So we definitely value their time and skills.

The truth is that when you are **removing a pain** away from somebody else, most likely, people are going to be **willing** to pay a lot of money for it. In that sense, if you don't remove a pain from somebody in the market place, there is **no sale.** That is the reason why, we are willing to pay so much to the doctors, because they are treating our **pain points** directly, and we are eager to pay a lot of money for their skills in return.

Therefore, you have to become very valuable in the market place or develop the skills, that is going to solve a lot of people' pain points when it comes to their businesses and their lives. People will value your time, depending on how well you **solve** their problems, and how good are the solutions that you are giving them, to **reduce their pain.**

Therefore, make sure, that you have or that you developed some tangible and practical skills, that are valuable in the market place. So that people **trade your time**, for their money, at the highest price or the highest rate.

The key here is to **add value** to your time, from the point of view of others, so that **they pay** a lot of money for your time and resources. Think about Michael Jordan, Will Smith, Lionel Messi or Cristiano Ronaldo and how **much money** do you think their time costs? People are willing to pay a lot of money to go and see these athletes and artist performing at their professional activities, not only because they love the very unique skills they have in their fields, but people also pay a lot of money to these extraordinary individuals because *people value* their time. And that is indeed, a wealth creation position to be in when *people value* your time, more than they value theirs. In that sense, *time is money*, especially when people are willing and able to pay you a lot of money for your time in exchange for your skills.

Make money while you sleep

The truth is that if you really want to make a lot of money, you will have to find a mechanism that will make you money while you *sleep*. That is the bottom line. There are many investment vehicles and products and services out there that can do this for you. Of course, they are difficult to catch, because otherwise, everybody will be conducting those types of investments. But the truth is that if you are making money 24/7, 365 days per year, you are in your way, to becoming a multimillionaire. We teach a few tactics for these purposes in chapter five. Make sure you read them carefully. Best of luck for you in your wealth creation and management process. Discipline and investment knowledge is what is going to get you there and always remember the principle number five of this book, which is know your timing when investing.

You have got to learn how to invest your time wisely but also your money. It would be a lot better if you begin the process of learning how to manage your wealth portfolio from a very early age, in order to capitalize from it, at a later date. Think about all of the hours that Michael Jordan spent at the basketball court. Most likely, he spent more time than any other kid on planet earth at the basketball court, because expert mastering of any kind of sport, does not comes only from the physical attributes that you may have, but they mostly come from discipline, consistency, passion, practice, commitment and a strong competitive drive that pushes you to become the best in the world at your one specific field.

The same mentality, discipline, and commitment need to be implemented when it comes to investing your money and your time. And always remember, *time is money*, spend it well. Also, if you can, be patient. Analyze very well every investment you are going to make. Just like Warren Buffett Says: **"The stock market is a device for transferring money from the impatient to the patient."** When people are looking for an urgent solution to their problem, and you have the solution, don't sell it for cheap. Don't give it for free either. If they need their solution now, they have to pay the prime prices for your products of your services.

Disclaimer: While I was going to add another critical chapter at the end of this book called "Network like a Billionaire," I realized that the topics of that chapter were not only extremely valuable but also, they should be available in a new single book by itself. If you want to purchase my new book, "Network Like a Billionaire," please do so in my online store at www.fabianavilastore.com, or you can get it at Amazon.com. We live in a digital age, and you must take advantage of that. Best of luck.

10 Principles of a Millionaire

Principle #1

"Arbitrage, Buy Low, Sell High"

Principle # 2

"Scale up your business"

Principle # 3

"Keep Your Cost Low"

Principle # 4

"Market and Advertise like a Millionaire".

Principle # 5

"Know Your Timing when Investing"

Principle # 6

"Leverage other people's skills and resources"

Principle # 7

"Stage time is wealth time"

Principle #8

"Money is Energy. Never give your energy for free".

Principle # 9

"Producing is better than Consuming"

Principle # 10

"Time is money"

Bibliography

[1] Klarmanite, 2014. Machiavelli's The Prince: On Virtue vs. Fortune – Part I
http://www.investingintheclassics.com/archives/36
[2]I.d

[3] Shopify.com, 2019. Understanding Dropshipping. Retrieved online from.
https://www.shopify.com/guides/dropshipping/understanding-dropshipping

[4] Lynda Banks, 2018. Direct & Indirect Sales Strategy
https://smallbusiness.chron.com/direct-indirect-sales-strategy-2208.html

[5] Susan Ward, 2018. Niche Market Definition for Business
https://www.thebalancesmb.com/niche-market-definition-for-business-2947188

[6] Unbounce.com, 2019. What is a landing page? https://unbounce.com/landing-page-articles/what-is-a-landing-page/

[7] Copywriting 101. https://www.copyblogger.com/copywriting-101/

[8] What is copywriting? https://www.awai.com/what-is-copywriting/

[9] Furhmann, 2018. 5 Top Investors Who Profited From The Global Financial
Crisis https://www.investopedia.com/financial-edge/0411/5-investors-that-are-both-rich-and-smart.aspx
[10] I.d
[12] I.d

[13] Suzanne Deffree -December 12, 2018. Apple IPO makes instant millionaires,
December 12, 1980 https://www.edn.com/electronics-blogs/edn-moments/4403276/Apple-IPO-makes-instant-millionaires--December-12--1980

[14] "Stock", word meaning, 2019. https://financial-dictionary.thefreedictionary.com/stock

[15]http://shodhganga.inflibnet.ac.in/bitstream/10603/70593/14/14_chapter%20
3.pdf

[16] Ally Financial Inc, 2018. What Is Option Trading? 8 Things to Know Before You
Trade. https://www.ally.com/do-it-right/investing/trading-options-for-beginners.

https://www.realtymogul.com/knowledge-center/article/what-cash-flow-investing

[17] Hugh McIntyre, 2018. These Are The 10 Highest-Grossing Tours Of
2018.https://www.forbes.com/sites/hughmcintyre/2018/12/06/these-are-the-10-highest-grossing-tours-of-2018/#6b350ef298f9

[18] Theory Of Relativity
https://www.allaboutscience.org/theory-of-relativity.htm

[19] Kagan, Julia, 2019. Compound Interest
https://www.investopedia.com/terms/c/compoundinterest.asp

Troy, Segal. Jun 21, 2018. What is the Goal of Real Estate Wholesaling? Retrieved from:https://www.investopedia.com/ask/answers/100214/what-goal-real-estate-wholesaling.asp

Rehabvaluator.com, 2018. Getting Started in Real Estate Wholesaling: What is Wholesaling and How it Works. Retrieved from:
https://rehabvaluator.com/content/wholesaling-101/how-real-estate-wholesaling-works/

www.ingramcontent.com/pod-product-compliance
Lightning Source LLC
Chambersburg PA
CBHW070932210326
41520CB00021B/6901